KNOWLEDGE AND SCIENCE

Knowledge and Science

H. J. KANNEGIESSER

First published 1977 by
THE MACMILLAN COMPANY OF AUSTRALIA PTY LTD
107 Moray Street, South Melbourne 3205
12 Berry Street, North Sydney 2060

Associated companies in
London and Basingstoke, England
New York Dublin Johannesburg Delhi

National Library of Australia
cataloguing in publication data

Kannegiesser, Henry Joseph.
Knowledge and science.

Index.
Bibliography.
ISBN 0 333 22960 6.

1. Dewey, John, 1859–1952.
2. Education – Philosophy.
I. Title.

370.1

Set in Monophoto Baskerville by
The Macmillan Company of India, Bangalore
Printed in Hong Kong

Contents

Preface

The term 'instrumentalist' has often been used in a derogatory fashion by modern philosophers to describe certain ideas about truth, meaning, and the function of scientific theories that do not really fit within the logical positivist approach to the philosophy of science which has been popular since the days of the Vienna Circle. And the philosophical position known as 'Instrumentalism' has frequently been criticised in recent times, traditionally by the logical positivists but more recently by those who call themselves 'Scientific Realists'. However, when the common criticisms of Instrumentalism are examined, it becomes evident that the 'instrumentalist position' criticised differs from critic to critic. As a result, it seemed essential to prepare a clear account of instrumentalism before embarking on a discussion of the role of the instrumentalist mode of thought in philosophy of science.

This proved to be no simple task however, and what eventually emerged from the author's research was the realisation that there is no instrumentalist position as such – that Instrumentalism, like many other philosophical doctrines, is better described as a complex and heterogeneous 'family' of loosely related ideas than as a unified and consistent set of concepts. Furthermore, it also became apparent that not all instrumentalist systems contained the same members of the 'family', and that the relationships among the family members differed from system to system.

Therefore, this book has four main aims. Firstly to support the contention that Instrumentalism is a 'family' of loosely related ideas and theories. Secondly, to put forward those ideas and theories which appear to the author to qualify as members of the instrumentalist family of concepts. Thirdly, to justify the choice of these ideas and theories. And fourthly, to examine the ramifications of the family concepts with a view to re-evaluating the worth of some of the traditional criticisms that have been made against them.

In the process, considerable emphasis is placed on the work of John

Dewey who was the foremost proponent of 'Instrumentalism' for the seventy years prior to 1950. Dewey is a difficult writer to study, partly because of the number of his publications and partly because his working life was so long. As a matter of practical expediency, this book examines only a small fraction of his work, and concentrates mainly on his writings about Inquiry, Knowledge, Truth, and Science. However, despite these limitations in the scope, two sets of problems still arose. Firstly, it was difficult to avoid a large amount of repetition because Dewey tended to treat his philosophy as one organic whole and secondly, many of Dewey's beliefs underwent some degree of modification between 1880 and 1952. Fortunately, however, the essentials of Dewey's views about those matters relevant to the theme of this book remained largely unaltered over the years, and it was usually possible to ignore the historical development of his thinking.

Finally, despite the restricted scope of this book, one worthwhile result is the placing of Dewey's philosophical and educational works in the broader context in which they were produced, with some attention being given to the controversies and historical factors which led to their development.

This preface would be incomplete without a word of thanks to Professor D. C. Phillips, Faculty of Education, Stanford University, for his helpful advice and his sympathetic understanding of the difficulties encountered during the course of this project.

H.K.

I
Instrumentalism as a Philosophy of Science

The search for knowledge is as old as the history of mankind. With the beginning of social grouping and the use of tools for richer satisfaction of daily needs the desire to know arose, since knowledge is indispensable for control of the objects of our environment so as to make them our servants.[1]

Instrumentalists tend to see themselves as belonging to an ancient tradition in philosophy. According to a number of instrumentalist writers, including Dewey[2] and Reichenbach,[3] man has always interacted with his environment and manipulated it to achieve security, comfort and prosperity. Consequently, they believe that man has always tended to assess the value of his scientific ideas and theories according to their success or failure in helping him control nature, because, from the beginning of history, he has been involved in a constant attempt to harness nature and improve his ability to manipulate his environment. And, what was more, he achieved impressive results very early in his career. He learnt to use fire, killed and domesticated animals, cultivated plants, extracted metals from ores, shaped wood, stone and bone to suit his purposes, and, to better achieve success, he devised and used tools which became ever more complex and efficient. As a result, he was forced to think analytically, to generalise, to make distinctions, to specify, and to classify, and, in general, to develop the intellectual tools considered essential to the scientist. For instance, if the hardest metal he had available from which to fashion his tools was bronze, it was important for him to know whether a particular piece of rock was limestone or granite. If it was limestone, he could reshape it and use it; if it was granite, it might well be useless. If he could not make the appropriate distinction, a valuable bronze tool would be blunted or broken, and, although time was plentiful, metal was precious. Or, if he lived in the arid regions of ancient Lydia, he had to learn to classify the plants around him. Vegetation was sparse, and if he did not use effectively what he had, his food supply dwindled, his stock died, and he perished. Again, if he lived in ancient Egypt,[4] his life depended in a number of ways upon the flooding of the Nile. Consequently, he developed astronomy and geometry. He used the sun and stars to tell him when the Nile was about to rise, and to give him the base line necessary to re-survey his fields after the flood. Geometry was a necessary adjunct to this need to survey.

> The historical origin of geometry, which goes back to the Egyptians, supplies one of the many instances in which intellectual discoveries have grown from material needs. The annual floods of the Nile which fertilised the soil of Egypt brought trouble to landowners; the border lines of their estates were destroyed every year and had to be re-established by means of geometrical measurements. The geographical and social conditions of their country, therefore, compelled the Egyptians to invent the art of surveying.[5]

In fact, Instrumentalists tend to believe that a study of history suggests that most of man's intellectual advancement in the field of science has been brought about as a response to problems, to resolve some doubt, or to fulfil some need. That is, problem solving, in this broad sense, would seem to have been one of the chief causes of man's climb from his original primitive state to his present highly civilised and complex existence.

Instrumentalists are not alone in this belief and there would seem to be a deal of 'truth' in what they have to say. Consequently, it is not surprising that the writings of the early Greek scientists, and particularly the members of the Hippocratic school of medicine, indicate that they held what has often been described as an instrumentalist view of the nature of knowledge. In particular, they argued strongly that in matters concerning nature one should be guided more by successful practice than by metaphysical postulates when developing one's ideas.[6] However, their instrumentalist/operationalist view of science died with the advent of the Platonic view of reality and the creation of the comprehensive and successful Aristotelean systems of biology, cosmology, politics, and philosophy. Although both Plato and Aristotle appear to have acknowledged the importance of gross experience,[7] and despite the fact that Aristotle's biology was obviously based on numerous acute observations, in both the Platonic and Aristotelean systems theoretical postulates and strong metaphysical assumptions clearly guided the formulation of the final theories. In fact, the reader is often left with the strong impression that the philosophical axioms were more important than the observational data. An excellent example is Aristotle's 'obvious' dichotomy between the heavens and the earth (because of the *perfection* of the one and the *imperfection* of the other) which dominated astronomical thinking from 300 B.C. to the time of Copernicus in the sixteenth century A.D.

For well-known social, historical, religious, and intellectual reasons,

Platonic philosophy became an integral part of our European heritage, and Aristotle's writings, or, more correctly, a wide variety of interpretations of Aristotle's writings, formed the basis of medieval science. As a result, the instrumentalist tradition lost popularity and, although a few scientists from the intervening period can be regarded as being in the tradition,[8] it was not until the nineteenth century that instrumentalism underwent a major revival. Since then, however, men such as Bernard, Peirce, Jevons, Stallo, Mach, Pearson, Boutroux, James, Hertz, Boltzman, Poincaré, Duhem, Ostwald, Meyerson, Cassirer, Dewey, Russell, Whitehead, Campbell, Bridgman, Sullivan, Reichenbach, Nagel, Toulmin, and Kuhn have given support to some or all of the basic postulates of instrumentalism.

Instrumentalism in its modern form probably dates from Peirce's work on meaning and the logic of science in the late nineteenth century.[9] His ideas were accepted by William James (the psychologist) who extended Peirce's work to include a somewhat controversial theory of truth. John Dewey further refined and modified the theories of Peirce and James, wove them into the philosophical system we now know as instrumentalism, and for most of the first half of the twentieth century popularised this system and attempted to apply its concepts and methods, not only to science, but also to ethics, education, and social problems generally. As a result, although Dewey is not strictly a philosopher of science, it would seem essential that his work be given a prominent place in any discussion of the development of an instrumentalist mode of thought in modern philosophy of science. His writings have influenced many American philosophers of this century (including philosophers of science of the stature of Cohen and Nagel), he is generally known as the 'father' of instrumentalism, and he was certainly the leading proponent of this philosophical attitude for some fifty years.

Another reason for discussing Dewey's work in some detail is the fact that modern writers often 'refute' instrumentalism by the device of over-simplifying it. Now, it is possible to characterise any philosophical position as being very simple and simplistic, and as capable of almost instant refutation, but in the case of instrumentalism this involves a gross distortion of a rather complex set of ideas. An example of such a 'refutation by over-simplification' is given by Popper, when he states that,

> Instrumentalism can be formulated as the thesis that scientific theories—the theories of the so-called pure sciences—are nothing but computation rules (or inference rules),[10]

and then proceeds to rebut this thesis in less than three pages. However, it is argued in Chapter 2 that instrumentalism is a group or 'family' of

interrelated concepts, and therefore that Popper's assumption that
instrumentalism can be reduced to a belief in a single defining
characteristic does not do justice to the instrumentalist approach to
science.

Instrumentalism has suffered extensively from this type of criticism
since its rebirth in the nineteenth century. As early as 1907, James noted
that the philosophical ideas of Messrs Schiller and Dewey had suffered
a hailstorm of contempt and ridicule, and suggested that, 'all rationalism has risen against them'.[11] He also suggested that pragmatism, and
particularly the pragmatic view of truth which is such an integral part
of the instrumentalist mode of thought, would run through the classic
stages of a theory's career. That is—

> First . . . a new theory is attacked as absurd; then it is admitted to be true,
> but obvious and insignificant; finally it is seen to be so important that its
> adversaries claim that they themselves discovered it.[12]

James felt that in 1907 the pragmatic doctrine of truth was then in the
first of these three stages, with symptoms of the second stage having
begun.[13] Since then, there is little doubt that strenuous attempts have
been made to demonstrate that many facets of the instrumentalist
position, though 'true', are insignificant or trivial.

An integral part of many of these attempts to belittle the importance
of instrumentalism has been the use of criticisms based on an
oversimplification of instrumentalist ideas. As a result, many critics of
instrumentalism have seriously distorted that mode of thought because,
for most Instrumentalists and particularly for Dewey, instrumentalism
was a subtle complex of ideas which could not be reduced to a simple
thesis. It did not assert that scientific theories are nothing but
computation or inference rules (Popper); which did not necessarily
deny (or affirm) the reality of theoretical entities (Maxwell, Smart); it
did not maintain a rigid observational/theoretical distinction (Sellars,
Smart); it did not discourage the use of abstractions and theories, and
hence restrict the possibilities of advances in science (McLaughlin); and
it was not necessarily based on a fixed set of observation statements
(Smart).[14]

Consequently, it would seem to be advisable to undertake a detailed
examination of the instrumentalist position, before discussing its role in
the philosophy of science. This task is somewhat complex, because
instrumentalism appears to be what Wittgenstein called a 'family' of
concepts. For example, the instrumentalist theme that man's interaction with nature and his attempts to control it are basic to an
understanding of the development of science leads: (a) to the idea that
scientific theories are, at least, instruments for the control and
intelligent manipulation of nature; (b) to a re-examination of expla-

nations of causation, deduction, and induction; (c) to the claim that knowledge is not fixed, and that it may not be possible for a participator in the environment being studied to obtain knowledge of 'absolute truth' (if such a concept is meaningful); (d) to the belief that no knowledge or system of knowledge is certain and, therefore, all knowledge is open to modification at any time; (e) to the suggestion that scientific laws should be looked upon more as probability statements or statistical regularities than as rigid, mechanical rules; (f) to an emphasis on the scientist as a member of society, and hence to a consideration of the influence of philosophical, psychological, religious, and cultural factors on the development of scientific theories and on the standard scientific methods of reporting, supporting, and defending such theories; and finally, (g) to the suggestion that a scientist may claim no more than that his conclusions are reasonable, that on the evidence available he is warranted in asserting them.

During the discussion of these matters in the remainder of the book, it becomes plain that many critics attempt to sharply separate instrumentalism from other philosophies of science. However, such a separation is not possible, because instrumentalists, realists, empiricists, idealists, positivists, (and others), have much in common. This fact is highlighted throughout the book, and arguments are also put forward to suggest that being an 'Instrumentalist' need not prevent one from also being a 'Realist'.

The fact that instrumentalism shares many of its fundamental ideas with other philosophies of science came about because the pragmatic mode of thought (which is shown in Chapter 2 to be an integral part of most instrumentalist systems) is not a philosophy, but is rather an attitude to philosophical questions or a method of approach to philosophical problems. As James argued in 'What Pragmatism Means', pragmatism implies—

> The attitude of looking away from first things, principles, 'categories', supposed necessities; and of looking towards last things, fruits, consequences, facts.[15]

Consequently, James felt justified in asserting that—

> Being nothing essentially new, it (pragmatism) harmonises with many ancient philosophical tendencies. It agrees with nominalism for instance, in always appealing to particulars; with utilitarianism in emphasising practical aspects; with positivism in its disdain for verbal solutions, useless questions and metaphysical abstractions.[16]

However, it must be noted that pragmatism did not reject *all* abstractions. As James himself said—

> Pragmatism has no objection whatever to the realising of abstractions so
> long as you get among particulars with their aid and they actually carry you
> somewhere.[17]

As a result, James saw his philosophical position as opposed to radical forms of rationalism and other systems which concentrated heavily on verbal solutions, a priori reasoning, fixed principles, closed systems, and absolutes, but as compatible with most other approaches to philosophy.[18] Further to this point, it is interesting to note that Peirce claimed that his philosophy of science had distinct realist tendencies, whereas Dewey, while strongly supporting Peirce's approach, refused to accept the belief that the theoretical entities of science could be real or, alternatively, that man could ever know that they were real, if they were real. These matters are neither simple nor straightforward, and are discussed at considerable length throughout the book. However, they are briefly mentioned here to highlight the common fallacies of treating instrumentalism firstly, as though it were a fully fledged philosophical system, and secondly, as though it were a radical departure from most other philosophies of science.

As a result of the problems mentioned above, the following discussion of instrumentalism examines a wide spectrum of the philosophy of science and its history. In the process, a re-appraisal is made of some of the distinctions currently accepted between instrumentalism and other schools in the philosophy of science, and, in particular, the common distinction which is made between the 'Instrumentalist' and the 'Realist' is discussed.

NOTES

1   Reichenbach, H. *The Rise of Scientific Philosophy*, Uni. of California Press, Berkeley, 1968, p. 5.
2   Dewey, J. *The Quest for Certainty*, Capricorn Books, G. Putnam's Sons, N.Y., 1960, Chapters 1 and 2.
3   Reichenbach, H. *op.cit.*, Chapter 2 and Chapter 8.
4   i.e. between 4500 B.C. and approximately 1000 B.C.
5   Reichenbach, H. *op. cit.*, p. 125
6   See Chapter 3 for details.
7   Although Plato denigrates sense experience in both the *Timaeus* and the *Republic*, he nevertheless accepted the belief that scientific theories must 'save the phenomena'. i.e. the 'phenomena' may not be disregarded altogether, even though capricious, ever changing, unreliable, and in need of 'salvation' by some form of ideal mathematical system. For further discussion see Dijksterhuis, E. *Mechanisation of the World Picture*, O.U.P., London, 1960, pp. 13ff.
8   e.g. Francis Bacon.

9   His classic paper 'How to Make our Ideas Clear' was published in 1878.
10 Popper, K. *Conjectures and Refutations*, Routledge and Kegan Paul, London, 1969, p. 111.
11 James, W. 'What Pragmatism Means' in Konvitz, M. and Kennedy, G. *The American Pragmatists*, Meridian books, N.Y., 1967, p. 38.
12 *ibid*, p. 45.
13 *ibid*.
14 These matters are discussed in Chapters 2, 3, 4, particularly pp. 69ff.
15 James, W. in Konvitz, M. & Kennedy, G. *op. cit.*, p. 33.
16 *ibid*.
17 *ibid* pp. 40–1.
18 *ibid* pp. 31–3.

2
The Philosophical Basis of Instrumentalism

> There is – the tendency to look for something in common to all the entities which we commonly subsume under a general term. – We are inclined to say that there must be something in common to all games, say, and that this common property is the justification for applying the general term 'game' to the various games; whereas games form a family the members of which have family likenesses. Some of them have the same nose, others the same eyebrows and others again the same way of walking; and these likenesses overlap.[1]

Instrumentalism is a collection of ideas loosely related to the theme that man is an organism interacting with his environment and manipulating it to his advantage. It has no well-defined boundaries, and it is quite possible for two Instrumentalists to deny one another's basic propositions but still be considered Instrumentalists. Peirce denied James' theory of truth, and even went so far as to re-name his philosophy 'pragmaticism' to dissociate himself from James' version of pragmatism, but there is little doubt that most writers on the history of philosophy would consider both Peirce and James to be two of the founders of modern instrumentalism. This 'looseness' in the meaning of philosophical doctrines was noted by Lovejoy, who pointed out that—

> The total body of doctrine of any philosopher or school is almost always a complex and heterogeneous aggregate . . . It is not only a compound but an unstable compound.[2]

He further suggested that the traditional 'isms' such as Idealism, Romanticism, Rationalism, Transcendentalism, Pragmatism, and so on are names of complexes, not simples—and of complexes in two senses,

> They stand, as a rule, not for one doctrine, but for several distinct and often conflicting doctrines held by different individuals or groups to whose way of thinking these appellations have been applied, either by themselves or in the traditional terminology of historians; and each of these doctrines, in turn, is

likely to be resolvable into simpler elements, often very strangely combined and derivative from a variety of dissimilar motives and historic influences.[3]

For reasons similar to those noted by Lovejoy, it is very difficult to develop an acceptable account of the complex of ideas known as Instrumentalism, and the writer is forced into a position where he must invoke something like Wittgenstein's 'family concept' of meaning. Wittgenstein, when discussing in the *Blue Book* what the different processes of 'expecting some one to tea' have in common, was forced to conclude that—

> The answer is that there is no single feature in common to all of them, though there are many common features overlapping. These cases of expectation form a family; they have family likenesses which are not clearly defined.[4]

He illustrated a different but related case in the *Brown Book*, when examining the meanings of expressions of possibility such as 'can' and 'to be able to'. He noted that although there is a vast net of family likenesses, there are certain characteristic features which appear in different combinations.[5]

The group of concepts known as instrumentalism falls somewhere between Wittgenstein's two examples. There does not seem to be any single feature common to all the systems that have been labelled 'instrumentalist', but among the characteristics of the family are certain features which, nevertheless, serve to mark off instrumentalism from other philosophies of science. Not all of these characteristics appear in every instrumentalist system, and those that do appear in more than one system, often appear in different combinations. Consequently, the problem of the selection of the appropriate features from the family network and the justification of what is eventually selected is enormously difficult and, for the sake of clarity, has been approached in two ways. Firstly, the present chapter attempts briefly to explore the philosophical basis of instrumentalism. That is, to put forward the group of ideas from which a modern Instrumentalist would be likely to select his beliefs, and to note some of the difficulties he would be forced to face. Some concepts, such as the pragmatic theory of meaning (which have long been accepted as a part of the instrumentalist creed) are merely noted and are not analysed in any detail, but other aspects of instrumentalism, such as the ontological status of theoretical entities, where there is some doubt, even among Instrumentalists, about what would count as an acceptable answer, are given a more detailed exposition.

The second approach, which is that taken in Chapter 3, is to trace the history of some of the main ideas that have been designated as instrumentalist, partly to justify their inclusion in the instrumentalist 'family' of concepts, partly to highlight the philosophical problems they

were designed to answer, and partly to support the thesis that John
Dewey, rather than being a radical innovator in philosophy, performed
more the role of a philosophical 'engineer' who took contemporary
ideas and welded them into a coherent framework which covered many
of the traditional areas designated as philosophy of science.

The Instrumentalist Family of Concepts

It was suggested in Chapter 1 that Instrumentalism arose as a
philosophical response to the successful fulfilment of human needs via
the techniques and processes of science and technology. Just as these
needs cover a wide spectrum of human activity, so the instrumentalist
family of concepts covers a wide spectrum of philosophy. So wide a
spectrum, in fact, that historians and critics rarely agree about what
Instrumentalism is. Consequently, the following account of the basic
concepts of Instrumentalism is based on an analysis of the writings of
John Dewey, supported by a synthesis of the opinions of four historians
of philosophy — Passmore, Copleston, White, and Thayer. These
sources suggest that the most important facets of the instrumentalist
creed are:

1   The suggestion that one of the more fruitful ways of looking at
    science is to consider it as resulting from the activities of a
    biological organism (man) interacting with its environment and
    manipulating it to achieve security, happiness, comfort and so on.[6]
2   A view of logic which suggests that the laws of deduction were
    developed in the context of scientific inquiry and are to be tested
    by their contribution to the overall efficiency of science.[7]
3   A pragmatic theory of meaning.[8]
4   A theory of truth which suggests that there is no ultimate, fixed
    truth and that what a scientist calls true is what has not (yet) been
    falsified.[9]
5   A theory of value which attempts to eliminate conflicts between
    science and ethics.[10]
6   An analysis of the process of thinking which sees thought as
    something instrumental and involving the modification of ex-
    perience. As a result, ideas are seen as intellectual tools and guides
    to practice.[11]
7   The theory that knowledge is the formulation of successful
    practice.[12]
8   The suggestion that scientific practice is a complex form of the
    process of inquiry, similar to common sense procedures but dealing
    with different subject matter and therefore concentrating on
    different methods.[13]

THE PHILOSOPHICAL BASIS OF INSTRUMENTALISM

9 The view that scientific theories are never absolute but are hypotheses in need of constant revision.[14]

10 The notion that relations rather than events are the basis of science because they are the only constants man can find in nature, where change appears to be the rule rather than the exception.[15]

11 The suggestion that scientific laws are more akin to statistical regularities than to inflexible, mechanical rules.[16]

12 An underlying assumption that method is more important than subject matter because while the latter is always open to modification and change, the former allows man to successfully manipulate his environment.[17]

Although each of the twelve 'members' of the instrumentalist 'family' has been labelled as typically instrumentalist at some stage in the history of science, it is certainly not the case that all (or even any) Instrumentalists would subscribe to all (or many) of these twelve concepts. As a result, one is forced to the conclusion that the instrumentalist family of concepts does not form a comprehensive or complete philosophical system, but rather functions as a philosophical foundation or archetype[18] from which an Instrumentalist might build an explanation of the current workings of science. Therefore, it is not surprising that the attempts of different Instrumentalists at different times to use different concepts from the instrumentalist 'family' to develop such an explanation have produced a wide variety of results. One of the purposes of this book is to indicate the relationships between these different attempts at devising a comprehensive philosophy of science and to note the problems which led to their rejection or modification. However, before beginning this task, it will be necessary to examine each member of the instrumentalist family or archetype in some detail.

Man, the Problem Solver

One proposition which is frequently accepted as a part of the various instrumentalist systems is the assertion that man is an intelligent and complex biological organism who continually interacts with his environment and in the process manipulates it to achieve security, comfort, knowledge, and so on. In fact, it is from this basic proposition that most instrumentalist doctrines derive their force. For example, it was for this reason that Dewey took a view of logic that was directly opposed to that of most of his predecessors.[19] He did not see the rules of logic as something fixed, immutable, and independent of man; or look on the traditional system of logic as the only method of achieving an intellectually acceptable result. Instead, he believed that the laws of

deduction were developed in the context of scientific inquiry, and were
to be tested by their contribution to the overall efficiency of science.[20] In
short, that logic is a description of those methods of inquiry that are
successful.[21]

> This doctrine [Dewey's theory of reflection or thought] implies, moreover,
> that logical theory in its usual sense is essentially a descriptive study; that is an
> account of the processes and tools which have actually been found effective in
> enquiry, comprising in the term 'inquiry' both deliberate discovery and
> deliberate invention.[22]

However, although Dewey's instrumentalist view of logic appears to be
a new way of looking at the subject, it is hardly as revolutionary a
concept as some commentators would seem to suggest.[23] For instance,
his assertion that logic is a description of those methods of inquiry that
are successful simply means that he believes logic describes the method
of reasoning we must use if we wish to avoid certain fallacies, to predict
accurately, and to reach conclusions that are in accord with experience.
That is, this approach would seem to reduce, in essence, if not in
emphasis, to the eighteenth/nineteenth century view of logic which
suggested that logic prescribed how we *should* think (if we are to avoid
certain fallacies, to predict accurately, and to reach conclusions which
are in accord with experience). In consequence, whether or not Dewey
offered a different logic may be a matter for debate, but most
commentators seem to agree that what he did do that was of merit was
to offer a new account of the old principles,[24] and to emphasise the
pragmatic function of logic. That is, Dewey reminded his age that man
discovered long ago that the world works in certain set ways, and if he
wanted to control and adapt nature, he would have to accord with
nature's patterns and reason in certain set ways.[25]

> Logical order is not a form imposed upon what is known; it is the proper form
> of knowledge as perfected. For it means that the statement of subject matter is
> of a nature to exhibit to one who understands it the premises from which it
> follows and the conclusions to which it points. As from a few bones the
> competent zoologist reconstructs an animal; so from the form of a statement
> in mathematics or physics the specialist in the subject can form an idea of the
> system of truths in which it has its place.[26]

There are, of course, difficulties in such an instrumentalistic view of
logic, and answers to questions such as, 'What is a method of inquiry?'
'What is a successful method of inquiry?' 'What is meant by the
statement "tested by their contribution to the overall efficiency of
science"?', are neither immediate nor obvious. However, since there are
numerous recent studies of instrumentalist logic available in current
literature,[27] these issues will not be pursued here.

Briefly then, an Instrumentalist will typically see the laws of logic as part of a successful method of problem solving (inquiry) which has evolved over the centuries, and will suggest that these laws are used as instruments to render intelligent the actions involved in inquiry. That is, the validity of logic is to be demonstrated by its success in assisting man to solve his problems, because, as Dewey frequently pointed out, logical theory is an account of the processes and tools which have been found effective in inquiry.[28]

> The distinctions and classifications that have been accumulated in 'formal' logic are relevant data; but they demand interpretation from the standpoint of use as organs of adjustment to material antecedents and stimuli. . . . All the typical investigatory and verificatory procedures of the various sciences indicate the ways in which thought actually brings to successful fulfilment its dealing with various types of problems.[29]

> The value of research for social progress; the bearing of psychology upon educational procedure; the mutual relations of fine and industrial art; the question of the extent and nature of specialisation in science in comparison with the claims of applied science; the adjustment of religious aspirations to scientific statements; the justification of a refined culture for a few in face of economic insufficiency for the mass; the relation of organisation to individuality – such are a few of the many social questions whose answer depends upon the possession and use of a general logic of experience as a method of inquiry and interpretation.[30]

Meaning

The history of modern instrumentalism is closely related to the development of pragmatism – a philosophical viewpoint which has its origins in the work of the American scientist and philosopher, C. S. Peirce, who was writing on theories of meaning and problems in the logic of science during the late nineteenth century. His ideas were later extended and developed by William James and John Dewey, who both tended to look upon instrumentalism as a set of broad philosophical principles which were useful to guide one's thinking about science. In this way, it closely resembled its parent, pragmatism, which was originally conceived as a *method* of philosophising[31] and, like pragmatism, instrumentalism has achieved permanence more as a suggestive body of ideas than as a school of thought.[32]

One of the more important members of this suggestive body of ideas was the instrumentalist concept or 'method' of meaning. This concept has been variously explained,[33] but basically it reverts to the proposition that the 'objects' which give rise to words and concepts lead to certain practical consequences, and it is differences in these 'cash values' that indicate differences in meaning.[34] As well, some Instrumentalists wish to make the further claim that the significance of an idea or concept is also dependent upon these practical consequences. For example, Peirce suggested that the injunction, 'By your fruits ye shall know them', is part of the ancestral history of pragmatism.[35] Or, to be more precise, he believed that,

> . . . if one can define accurately all the conceivable experimental phenomena which the affirmation or denial of a concept could imply, one will have therein a complete definition of the concept . . . [36]

and, more generally,

> The entire intellectual purport of any symbol consists in the total of all general modes of rational conduct which, conditionally upon all the possible different circumstances and desires, would ensure upon the acceptance of the symbol.[37]

Peirce claimed that he based his method upon scientific practice, and he looked upon it as a means of clarification and analysis of concepts. From his point of view, a typically instrumentalist response to an appeal to give the meaning of a particular term would be the assertion that statements of the form 'This is x' may be translated to 'If an operation O is performed on this, then E is experienced'. That is, instead of the conditional being used to clarify the meaning of a concept, he claimed that the conditional *was* the meaning of the concept. For instance, 'This is hard' may be translated to (means) 'If this is scratched by a piece of steel (quartz, diamond . . .), it will show no mark'.[38] In practice this theory of meaning was perhaps not as precise as Peirce would have wished, and is not entirely satisfactory even when considerably elaborated and hedged about with restrictions[39] (e.g., the meanings of some scientific terms such as gene; quark; π, θ, and τ mesons; etc. are heavily theory-bound, and here practical consequences are of considerably less importance than theoretical relations). However, the pragmatic method has proved a useful device for clarifying the meanings of words and concepts, and is often used as such by the scientist. For example, in answer to the question, 'What is meant by the term acid?', a chemist will usually begin by replying, 'If a substance is an acid, it will turn litmus paper red, react with a base to produce a salt, etc.', and go on to produce as complex a definition as his current situation warrants. Now, there is no doubt that there are other ways a chemist may define an acid besides citing a series of possible physical operations, and it is true that there are scientific concepts that are difficult (if not impossible) to define in such a way. Nevertheless, the instrumentalist/operationalist theory of meaning has long had a prominent place in scientific practice. As a result, many Instrumentalists have felt obliged to incorporate some form of a pragmatic theory of meaning into their system of thought, but, as would be expected, have therefore had to accept a host of philosophical problems.

Truth – Introduction

The nature of truth is another traditionally difficult area in the philosophy of science and one of the more popular instrumentalist solutions, although analogous to standard scientific practice, is still considered controversial. Theoretically the scientist accepts no scientific theory as final,[40] and most Instrumentalists accept as an article of faith that there is no ultimate fixed truth in the traditional sense.[41] They tend to agree with the physicist, Campbell, that—

> A proposition is true in so far as it states something for which the universal assent of all mankind can be obtained.[42]

Furthermore, some go as far as to suggest that if there is an ultimate reality or antecedent Being, it is highly likely that man will never know it.[43]

Instrumentalists normally present three main arguments to support their position:

a   As James pointed out in 'Pragmatism's Conception of Truth',[44] although correspondence with reality may well be the proper criterion for truth, in practice, how may we know when our ideas do correspond with reality? What do we mean by correspondence? or reality?

In applying Peirce's criterion of meaning to the traditional correspondence theory of truth, James reached the conclusion that the practical consequences of such correspondence would not uniquely lead us to realise that the correspondence had taken place, i.e. that we would not know when we were in the possession of 'truth'.[45]

Consequently, while not rejecting out of hand the correspondence theory of truth, James looked elsewhere for a useful criterion of truth and found it in pragmatism.

> True ideas are those that we can assimilate, validate, corroborate and verify. False ideas are those that we can not . . . Truth *happens* to an idea. It *becomes* true, is *made* true by events. Its verity *is* in fact an event, a process: the process namely of its verifying itself, its *verification*. Its validity is the process of its valid-*ation*.[46]

> Truth in science is what gives us (Scientists) the maximum possible sum of satisfactions, taste included; but consistency both with previous truth and with novel fact is always the most imperious claimant.[47]

b The history of science suggests a progression from primitive and barely useful theories to more 'correct' theories which allow the environment to be understood more completely and manipulated more expertly. The progression from Aristotelean physics to Newtonian physics and from Newtonian physics to modern physics is usually cited as the classical example. As this improvement, development, or growth has been evidenced in every branch of science over the past six thousand years, it has been suggested that there is some meaning in the comparison that is often made between the refinement of scientific ideas and the relative frequency theory probability. That is, scientific theories gradually improve and approach (but may never reach) a perfect correspondence with reality, just as the more times an unbiased coin is tossed, the more likely a relative frequency of fifty per cent heads will be approached (but may never be reached). For instance, in the case of Peirce, Thayer suggests that

> The convergence to truth or a limit of probable and statistical methods 'if persistently applied' and 'in the long run' are characteristic features of Peirce's philosophical view of enquiry and knowledge.[48]

and Peirce himself says that,

> The true guarantee of the validity of induction is that it is a method of reaching conclusions which, if it is persisted in long enough, will assuredly correct any error concerning future experience into which it may temporarily lead us.[49]

For Instrumentalists, the consequences of this position are that science has always been in a state of change, will always be in a state of change, but is all the time approaching 'truth' in the traditional sense of the term. Also, as Thayer has observed, from the point of view of Peirce (and many other Instrumentalists),

> The scientific method then is self applicable and self corrective in exactly the way that probable and inductive methods are . . .[50]

c The recognition of man as a biological organism interacting with his environment, as a participator rather than a spectator, would seem to suggest that there will be some (perhaps many) situations, at least in the micro world, where 'absolute' knowledge would be theoretically impossible because the intrusion of man or his instruments will change the original situation.[51] The usual example is the famous (or infamous) Heisenberg Uncertainty Principle which infers that one cannot obtain a precise simultaneous measurement of both the position and velocity of an electron because the act of observation alters the situation.[52]

Truth – the Instrumentalist View

As a result of arguments such as those given above, although an Instrumentalist may accept the statement that a belief would be 'true' if it represented nothing but reality, he tends to prefer definitions of truth such as the following:

1 *S is true* translates to *If you believe or accept statement S, then certain satisfactory experiences ensue.*[53]
2 *S is true* means that acting on S allows us to deal more adequately with experience.[54]
3 A scientific theory is true if satisfactory results ensue from the acceptance of and action upon such a theory.[55]
4 This belief is warranted (true) because it is an effective solution to that problem.[56]
5 Truth in science means scientific acceptability. That is, theory T is true if most experts in the field accept and use T.[57]
6 Statement S is true if S has been accepted by relevant experts and has not been falsified.[58]

Despite the fact that Instrumentalists usually predicate such statements of propositions rather than of things or facts, all such attempts at defining truth have led to numerous philosophical problems. What is a 'satisfactory experience'? What does 'deal more adequately with experience' mean? What are 'satisfactory results', and so on? Although the Instrumentalist can normally offer what he considers to be satisfactory answers to these questions in terms of a movement from an unsettled to a settled situation, or of predictability, or of falsification, or any mixture of these three criteria, any alleged failure on his part to provide complete answers rarely bothers him because in actual practice, as far as the scientists working on a given problem are concerned, there is little doubt about what would count as an effective solution to that problem. The term 'scientific acceptability' has definite meaning in reference to scientific practice.

For example, quantum theory has now gained scientific acceptability, whereas in the nineteen twenty's it had not; the phlogiston theory was not scientifically acceptable after Lavoisier's formulation of the oxygen theory of combustion; and so on.

Consequently, although the Instrumentalist must concede the point that the fact that most scientists accept theory A does not necessarily make theory A 'true' in the traditional sense, he believes that the acceptance of theory A by most scientists would seem to go some way to providing a justification for holding that theory A is at least the 'most reasonable' belief, that there must be some good reason for so much common consent.[59] However, despite the Instrumentalist's claim that he can offer a workable solution to this problem, the concept of truth has remained a controversial area in most instrumentalist philosophies.[60]

Value

Another longstanding problem for philosophers has been the task of including in the one philosophical framework interpretations of science and ethics that are not in conflict.[61] Instrumentalists have not been idle in this field. Dewey spent most of his life attempting to build such a framework[62] and, in more recent times, Reichenbach was involved in a similar exercise.[63] Dewey firmly believed that

> The reconstruction (in philosophy) to be undertaken is not that of applying 'intelligence' as something ready made. It is to carry over into any inquiry into human and moral subjects the kind of method (the method of observation, theory as hypothesis, and experimental test) by which understanding of physical nature has been brought to its present pitch.[64]

The result of Dewey's 'reconstruction' was the suggestion that something has value if and only if enjoying or liking it is the outcome of an intelligently controlled action. He laid great stress on the final three words, *intelligently, controlled,* and *action.* Now, there are overtones of utilitarianism in this approach, and Dewey would seem to be suggesting that, 'This is good' translates to, 'If Operation O is performed on this, E is experienced'; where 'O' and 'E' must be defined according to the situation and the philosophical background of the agents concerned.[65]

> This issue (i.e. defining value) involves nothing less than the problem of the directed reconstruction of economic, political and religious institutions.[66]

> Moral goods and ends exist only when something has to be done. The fact that something has to be done proves that there are deficiencies, evils in the existent situation. . . . Consequently, the good of the situation has to be discovered, projected and attained on the basis of the exact defect and trouble to be rectified.[67]

This brief and oversimplified account of Dewey's ideas distorts somewhat his rather complicated views on ethics, but serves to indicate the type of approach taken by Instrumentalists in the early decades of the twentieth century. Such theories have not been enormously successful, and, with other utilitarian type theories, have been severely criticised by many philosophers, including McCloskey[68] (1965) and Warnock[69] (1967). However, putting aside the question of the worth of such theories, this type of approach does serve as a reminder of the importance of the instrumentalist view of the nature of man.[70] Such matters may not initially appear relevant to a discussion in the philosophy of science, but, in the case of the Instrumentalist, may not be ignored, because his views about the nature of man have so heavily influenced his approach to what he considers one of the most important *human* activities — science. To recapitulate, the Instrumentalist tends to see man (*a*) as a social animal, one of whose dominant characteristics is a search for security;[71] (*b*) as analogous to a biological organism interacting with its environment, which, because of a desire for equilibrium, it manipulates to its advantage,[72] and hence (*c*) as a participator in the world rather than as an observer of the world.[73]

> Only that which has been organised into our dispositions so as to enable us to adapt the environment to our needs and to adapt our aims and desires to the situation in which we live is really knowledge.[74]

In other words, knowledge (of which science is a branch), rather than being truly objective, is very much man-dependent.

Thought

Interpretations of man's role in nature, such as those given above, have often led Instrumentalists into philosophical disputes. In particular, Scientific Realists (e.g., McLaughlin)[75] strongly disagree with their approach, and usually prefer to remove man altogether from explanations of the workings of nature.

However, despite the problems it engenders, the Instrumentalist usually prefers to retain his anthropocentric position, because it is from his 'man as a participator' model that he derives many of his theories about thinking and ideas, and hence about science. For example, an Instrumentalist will usually view thinking as a process of inquiry, that is, as a response by man to some disturbing element in the total context in which he finds himself, as something instrumental, and as leading to security and control of the environment.[76]

> Simple or complicated, relating to what to do in a practical predicament or what to infer in a scientific or philosophic problem, there will always be the two sides; the conditions to be accounted for, dealt with, and the ideas that are suppositions for interpreting and explaining the phenomena.[77]

Therefore, to an Instrumentalist, thinking involves the modification of experience, that is, experimentation. Dewey highlighted this fact in his formal analysis of the process of thinking. He suggested five main stages.[78]

1 The doubtful situation which suggests the problem e.g. the realisation, for a believer in the phlogiston theory, that calxes are heavier than the original metal.
2 The analysis of the doubtful situation, to define the problem and

determine what observations, etc. are relevant to the problem (i.e. *selection* of data).

> e.g. *Problem*: Most substances when burnt lose weight, but metals when heated increase weight. Why?
>
> *Relevant matters*: Role of air? Role of fire? Gases given off? Gases absorbed? Total weight before combustion? Total weight after combustion? And so on.

3 The formulation of hypotheses (ideas) which are blue-prints of operations to be performed to solve (perhaps) the problem.[79]

> e.g. Lavoisier's hypothesis that 'oxygen' combines with metals when they are heated.

4 The testing and revision of the hypotheses. This may be a very involved process, and include extensive alterations to the original hypotheses.

> e.g. Lavoisier's experiments on the oxides of mercury.

5 If 4 is successful, the problem is solved and the original doubt removed.

> e.g. Lavoisier's conclusion that combustion is a form of oxidation.

Although most Instrumentalists appear to accept a scheme of this type, they do not normally look upon it as a description of an invariable process which thinking always follows, and make some important qualifications, viz. :

a A distinction must be made between actual thinking and logic. For instance—

> **1** The steps of the thinking process as set out above have been formalised for the purpose of discussion. That is, what has been given is an account of the logical steps involved. However, in any real situation the number of steps may be more or less than five, and need not follow one another in a set order.[80]
>
> > In conclusion we point out that the five phases of reflection that have been described represent only in outline the indispensable traits of reflective thinking. In practice two of them may telescope, some of them may be passed over hurriedly, and the burden of reaching a conclusion may fall mainly on a single phase, which will then require a seemingly disproportionate development. No set rules can be laid down on such matters.[81]
>
> However, in essence, the instrumentalist claim appears to be that, despite the particular differences in procedures from situation to situation, thinking involves moving from problem to hypothesis, then from hypothesis via some sort of verification or vindication to a conclusion.

We may carry our account further by noting that *reflective* thinking, in distinction from other operations to which we apply the name of thought, involves (1) a state of doubt, hesitation, perplexity, mental difficulty, in which thinking originates, and (2) an act of searching, hunting, inquiring, to find material that will resolve the doubt, settle and dispose of the perplexity.[82]

2 The processes used to arrive at a conclusion differ from those used to explain, or support, or defend the conclusion.

It follows from these contrasts that thought is looked at from two different points of view . . . logical form and existent, or psychological, process . . . it [logic][83] sets forth forms into which the result of actual thinking is thrown in order to help test its worth.[84]

Logical forms such as one finds in a logical treatise do not pretend to tell *how* we think or even how we *should* think. No one ever arrived at the idea that Socrates, or any other creature, was mortal by following the form of the syllogism. If, however, one who has arrived at that notion by gathering and interpreting evidence wishes to expound to another person the *grounds* of his belief, he might use the syllogistic form and would do so if he wished to state the proof in its most compact form. A lawyer, for example, who knows in advance what he wants to prove . . . and who wishes to impress others with it, is quite likely to put his reasonings into syllogistic form. In short, these forms apply not to *reaching* conclusions, not to *arriving* at beliefs and knowledge, but to the most effective way in which to set forth what has already been concluded, so as to convince others (or oneself if one wishes to recall to mind its grounds) of the soundness of the result.[85]

In effect, Dewey was suggesting what has more recently been asserted by Popper[86] and Reichenbach,[87] that there is no universally accepted theory of discovery, and that there are differences between the logics of explanation, support, and defence. For example, the methods of exposition of a science text book,[88] of Harvey,[89] and of Darwin,[90] are notably different.

b There is no necessary movement from one step to another of the formalised process of thinking. For instance, there is the abductive 'gap' noted in **a 2** between step 2 (definition of the problem) and step 3 (formulation of an explanatory hypothesis). As well, step 4 (testing and revision of the hypothesis) may lead to the rejection of the original hypothesis, or even to a reformation of the original problem, and hence to a reversion to step 1 (the doubtful situation), before the process is finally completed and step 5 is reached (the problem is solved).

The acceptance of a conceptual background, such as that sketched above,[91] may lead to a departure from the traditional approach to some philosophical concepts. For instance, in the context of the processes of science, abduction may be looked upon as the process whereby an observer/participator moves from the realisation that he is involved in a doubtful situation to his formulation of an hypothesis to solve the problem generated by that situation (steps 1 to 3). As well, deduction and induction may be looked upon as basically concerned with steps 3 to 5, that is, with the justification or confirmation of an hypothesis.[92] Consequently, instrumentalists often claim that science, the most 'successful' form of thinking, laid the foundations for logic[93] or, alternatively, that logic is another example of a highly successful scientific method.[94]

Another consequence of the instrumentalist conceptual background is that ideas (concepts, hypotheses, theories, etc.) can easily be interpreted as intellectual tools and guides to practice,[95] that is, as instruments or plans which determine the operations that man may use to transform and manipulate nature to serve his various purposes. And this is precisely the role that an instrumentalist like Dewey would want them to fill for a wide variety of reasons closely related not only to his fundamental beliefs about man, but also to his beliefs about science, scientific method, and the relationship of science to human values.[96]

It should also be noted that the Instrumentalist commonly views ideas as plans for *possible* action.[97] That is, action need not necessarily follow the formulation of an idea, but when man tests an idea, he does so in terms of practice, i.e., by what is to be done if that idea is to be accepted as correct, according to the consequences of acting upon that belief, and so on.[98] In many ways, this philosophical position is merely an extension of Kant's suggestion that ideas have a regulative function in reason,[99] and, as might be expected, such a reformulation of a traditional problem area of philosophy is not without its own difficulties. However, these difficulties are not insuperable for those philosophers who, like Reichenbach, while holding that ideas are basically intellectual instruments, will leave open the possibility that they may also be 'more than' plans for possible action, and accept that it is conceivable that there may be circumstances wherein it is appropriate to investigate their 'truth' or 'falsity', even if such circumstances do not appear to occur in practice.[100]

Another possible consequence of the instrumentalist position is the suggestion that scientific knowledge is successful practice. That is, science basically consists of successful ideas—ideas which have been fully tested by experiment and experience. Such ideas are the results of inquiry, and, as such, imply a strong connection between theory and practice. Theory arises from practice, and practice is used to test theory.[101]

Scientific Theories

Now that some of the various instrumentalist attitudes to science have been noted, it is possible to discuss the instrumentalist approach to the role of scientific theories in more detail. As might be expected from what was said at the beginning of the chapter, there is no unique instrumentalist attitude to scientific theories, but most instrumentalists tend to look upon the theories of science as being tentative and constantly in need of revision. They advance numerous reasons for this belief, some of which have been already mentioned, and some which it is appropriate to introduce at this juncture.

It has already been noted that one of the concepts most often associated with instrumentalism is the idea that science is a mode of thinking about things which was developed so that man might manipulate them to desired ends, that is, to lead to the operational control of nature. An analogous notion is the idea that scientific practice is a complex form of the process of inquiry, similar to common-sense procedures but dealing with different subject matter and therefore concentrating on different methods.[102] If this attitude is taken, science tends to be seen as a continuing process of inquiry which is both based on gross experience and verified by it; that is, its theories begin with some practical problem and are tested in action by the practical results they lead to.

These matters raise a variety of philosophical problems, some of which require considerable discussion. However, such discussions are not appropriate here and are postponed until Chapters 4 and 5. For present purposes, it is sufficient to tentatively accept the proposition that many Instrumentalists[103] subscribe to a position similar to that noted above, and to proceed to an examination of the effects of this position on their attitude to scientific theories. By looking upon science as a continuing process of inquiry, Instrumentalists obtain support for their contention that science and scientific theories can never be absolute because—

1 Man is an integral part of his environment and changes in his behaviour produce changes in the environment, thereby complicating his attempts to know the environment qua environment. For this reason, and for those cited on page 17, most Instrumentalists refuse to entertain the possibility of absolute truth;

2 The scientist never uses the whole of the observational evidence available to him, but heavily selects those facets (data) which appear to him to be relevant to his problem;[104]

3 As Bernard says in *An Introduction to the Study of Experimental Medicine*,

chapter 5, there is always the possibility of the discovery of new 'facts' which may make current theories untenable.[105]

It is evident that the Instrumentalist has a variety of reasons for looking on scientific theories as being tentative and in need of constant revision but, because of the undoubted success of science (as a method of control of nature and as the sine qua non of modern technology), he usually accepts current theories as 'true' until they are proved 'false' (that is, cease to lead to the solutions of problems) or until a 'more correct' theory is devised.[106] 'More correct' in the sense that the new theory would be more successful than the old because it **1** explains more facts than the old theory; or **2** includes the old theory as a consequence of, or a special case of, or as a first approximation to the new theory; or **3** proves more fruitful than the old theory and has wider ramifications, relates hitherto unconnected theories, reveals new facts, and so on.[107] The spirit of this approach is perhaps captured by Dewey's use of the phrase 'warranted assertability' to describe the status of conclusions/theories which he considered were 'satisfactory' results of inquiry.[108]

From this point of view, the classical example of a more successful theory replacing one that had previously proved adequate is the replacement of Newtonian physics by a physics based on Einsteinian relativity.[109] Among other things, the post-Einstein physics explained the hitherto inexplicable difference between the predicted and actual advance in perihelion of Mercury[110] (i.e. explained more facts than the previous theory); gave results which demonstrated that the Newtonian transformation equations are almost identical with the Lorentz transformation equations, when the relative velocity of the reference frames is small compared with that of light[111] (i.e. included the previous theory as a special case of the new theory); and finally, related electromagnetic theories to optical phenomena, and led to the discovery that matter and energy are related by the equation $E = mc^2$ (i.e. proved more fruitful than the old theory).

Scientific Objects and Relations

Instrumentalists tend to see the subject matter of science as being more concerned with the relations between events than with the events themselves. They have two main reasons for this approach:

1 Because nature is in a constant state of flux, it is easier to recognise constants and uniformities among relations than among events. Hence, man looks upon relations as the more important, because he can use these recognised uniformities to control nature in his constant search for security and comfort.[112]

2   Because relativity theory eliminated the notion of absolute space, time, and motion as physical existences, it strongly encouraged the belief that space, time, and motion (and most other scientific concepts) designate relations of events.[113]

Instrumentalists further suggest that it is from the observation of visible (measurable) relations such as velocity and weight that the scientist infers the hidden operations (e.g. behaviour of sub-atomic particles) which he uses to explain and eventually manipulate his environment. A very crude analogy similar to those developed by Dewey is that between the physicist and the doctor.[114] The suggestion is that by using current theories and, among other data, observations of the behaviour of particles in a Wilson cloud chamber to attempt to explain atomic structure, the physicist is behaving in much the same way as the doctor, who uses current theory plus observations of pulse, blood pressure, bodily excretions, etc., to make inferences about the workings of internal (unobservable) organs.

When scientific practice is looked at in this way, scientific objects (atoms, electrons, positrons, quarks, genes, etc.) need not be considered real in the sense of having actual, existential import (but of course may be treated as real in this sense). What is important to the Instrumentalist is not questions about the existential status of scientific objects, but questions about whether or not the theories which include reference to these scientific objects are successful, and psychologically satisfying to the appropriate body of scientists. If a theory proves useful to scientists, does not conflict too drastically with current knowledge, and is of a type that is 'believable' in the light of current scientific attitudes and beliefs, most instrumentalists are not too concerned about the type of 'existence' of every entity postulated by the theory.

For example, the two most famous early Instrumentalists, Peirce and Dewey, held opposing views about the existence of the theoretical objects of science. Peirce's attitude to 'reals' is very similar to that of the modern realist,[115] and diametrically opposed to Dewey's assertion that electrons, etc. cannot be individual, existential objects.[116] However, this disagreement about the existential status of scientific objects was not considered important enough to prevent Dewey from borrowing heavily from Peirce's general philosophy, and using it as the basis for many of his ideas about scientific method.[117]

This ambivalence on the part of instrumentalists is often criticised and held up to ridicule, but the practice of scientists tends to support the instrumentalist approach. For instance, the authors of a well-known physics text-book clearly demonstrate a lack of concern for the existential status of theoretical entities when, after making use of the concept of the traditional 'Newtonian' atom (perfectly hard, perfectly elastic, etc.,) for their explication of the kinetic theory of gases,[118] they proceed to discuss atomic structure and see no contradiction or conflict of ideas in stating that—

> In the quantum mechanics it is more difficult to form a mental picture of what an atom is like. The modern theoretical physicist does not demand such a picture; rather he works with the somewhat diffused density distributions of electron charge in the atom.[119]

Charge Density

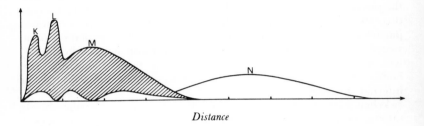

Distance

Charge distribution in potassium as a function of the distance from the centre of the atom.[120]

Another example from quantum theory concerns Schrödinger's ψ function. Although scientists are still undecided about the actual physical interpretation of the ψ function[121] (that is, whether a physical interpretation of the ψ function is possible and, if such an interpretation is possible, what 'type' it should be, what 'picture' it should evoke), they continue to use quantum theory and have based much of modern physics upon its postulates.

Such examples of a lack of concern by practicising scientists about the existential status of theoretical entities abound in science, so it would seem that questions about the status of theoretical entities are a problem only for those few instrumentalists who, like Dewey, refuse to allow that any such entities may be individual, existential objects. A sophisticated instrumentalist approach such as that noted by Nagel,[122] would see no inconsistency in claiming that some 'theoretical' entities are 'real', but that some would seem, on current interpretation, to be better described merely as convenient mental constructs, e.g. the so called 'point-masses' that perfectly obey Newton's second law of motion.

Now, the instrumentalist concern about current scientific practice has often been criticised because it allegedly leads to a pre-occupation with the practical and concrete, and encourages a neglect of the abstract and theoretical aspects of science.[123] In fact, however, the reverse is the case, because one important result of the mode of thought outlined above is that an Instrumentalist will usually encourage, rather than discourage, scientists to use abstractions and mathematics as much as possible. Firstly, because most Instrumentalists do not feel obliged to seek a physical interpretation of all (or any) theoretical terms and, secondly, because theories developed using such methods usually prove to be widest ranging, most useful, and most efficient.[124]

> . . . the things of our ordinary experience are fragmentary, casual, unregulated by purpose, full of frustrations and barriers. In the language previously used, they are problematic, obstructive, and challenges to thought. By ignoring for a time their concrete and qualitative fullness, by making abstractions and generalisations, we ascertain certain basic relations, upon which occurrence of the things experienced depend. We treat them as mere events, that is, as changes brought about in a system of relationships, ignoring their individualising qualities. But the qualities are still there, are still experienced, although as such they are not the objects of knowledge. But we return from abstractive thought to experience of them with added meaning and with increased power to regulate our relations to them.[125]

One consequence of this emphasis on the use of abstractions and mathematics, is the instrumentalist view of scientific laws. This view suggests that such laws should be considered more as statistical regularities and probability statements (Dewey)[126] or as inference licences (Toulmin),[127] than as inflexible mechanical rules. As shall be seen in Chapter 3, this reaction against a mechanistic explanation of scientific laws was part of a wider and more general movement in philosophy against the mechanistic modes of thought that had been popular since the seventeenth century. Scientists in particular, from at least the time of Mach in the middle decades of the nineteenth century, began to question the basic assumptions which had underlain the scientific thinking of their predecessors, and there developed a tendency to suggest what might loosely be termed 'conventionalist' interpretations of science.[128]

The last point of interest here, is to note that the instrumentalist emphasis on scientific practice tended to lead to a lack of concern about the philosophical problems of causality, mainly because there was a tendency to look upon any principle of causality as being essentially functional in character.[129] That is, it was the practical application of any such principle that was important, not the theoretical difficulties, because the latter were simply irrelevant to the practical success of the principle.

The Primacy of Method

As might be expected from what has already been said, the Instrumentalist is inclined to emphasise method rather than subject matter. The usual argument is that subject matter is never wholly fixed, is never infallible,[130] and is always changing; whereas an appropriate method, consistently applied, allows the successful manipulation of the environment.[131] Dewey suggested that, particularly in science, the use of an appropriate publicly described method allows all men to reach the same conclusion.[132] Peirce argued that the basic elements in the system of empirical knowledge are the methods that are employed, the 'habits' of inference used.[133] And Farrington maintains that intelligence should be measured by the success of the methods used by the agent, that understanding implies the ability to act consciously to achieve a desired end.[134] However, there is an important objection which may be raised against this point of view. Surely it is the case that *both* subject matter and method have been tested during previous inquiries and, just as a 'fact' today may prove to be a 'mistake' tomorrow, so a method that has been found to be reliable in the past may, nonetheless, fail in some future inquiry.[135] Consequently, apart from a subjective preference for one or the other, there would appear to be no more cogent reasons for the Instrumentalist's emphasis on method than there was for the traditional emphasis on subject matter.

Discussion

Throughout this chapter, it has become increasingly obvious that the instrumentalist family of concepts spreads over a considerable area of philosophy, and the name instrumentalism is used to cover a wide variety of sometimes conflicting ideas. Consequently, the commentator's task is extremely difficult because problems noted for Instrumentalist A who subscribes to concepts 1, 2, 3, 4[136] of the Instrumentalist family need not be problems for Instrumentalist B who subscribes to family concepts number 1, 5, 8, 9, and so on. As Lovejoy noted in *The Thirteen Pragmatisms and Other Essays*:

> It is true . . . that pragmatism also means instrumentalism. But . . . what has been called pragmatism is . . . a medley of diverse logical motives. Some of these I believe to be actually incompatible with one another. Most of them have on occasion been put forward separately and disconnectedly by pragmatist writers. Yet it cannot be denied that several of them are capable of being harmonised.[137]

A possibly misleading but somewhat illuminating analogy is that with the biologist's concept of the evolutionary effects of a stretched genetic pool. For example, the English crow is similar to and can breed with the French crow, the French crow is similar to and can breed with the German crow, and so on across Europe to the Russian and Siberian crows. However, the Siberian crow is not at all similar to the English crow and cannot breed with it. As a result, if the intervening varieties were to suddenly die out, then, according to current biological practice, the English and Siberian crows would have to be considered as different species.

A similar process appears to have occurred with the development of the instrumentalist family of concepts. As a result, as was noted earlier in this chapter,[138] only one of the twelve concepts put forward as members of the instrumentalist family, the assumption that science is a product of the interaction of man with his environment and his manipulation of that environment to achieve security, comfort, etc. (concept 1), has regularly appeared as a part of the many different instrumentalist systems which have been suggested over the past hundred years. The reasons for this state of affairs were twofold:

a   Modern instrumentalism evolved from a variety of different philosophical 'parents' as part of a more general nineteenth century reaction against the early mechanistic view that there were in nature certain fixed entities which obeyed certain fixed laws in a perfect manner, and that the role of science was to uncover those laws, rigidly define these entities, and so on.[139]

b   The idea that science is a product of the interaction of man with his environment was the only instrumentalist concept which was compatible with almost all of these 'parents'. That is, any argument among instrumentalists was likely to be about how this interaction influenced ideas in science, rather than about whether such interaction would lead man to want to investigate the fundamental workings of nature, and hence indulge in what we call scientific activity.

Besides concept 1, there was one other member of the instrumentalist family of concepts which, while not receiving universal assent among Instrumentalists, was compatible with many of the parent philosophies. That was the notion that scientific theories need not necessarily describe 'reality' but may always be regarded as convenient intellectual tools which help man control his environment. However, most of the remaining instrumentalist concepts appealed to a more restricted audience. For instance, although some Instrumentalists would agree that scientific theories were mere conventions, and/or that such theories should be treated as leading principles rather than premises, and/or that scientific laws are statistical regularities, and/or that science presupposes the possibility of an observed/unobserved, real/unreal dichotomy, it is certainly not the case that all Instrumentalists would subscribe to all of these beliefs.[140]

Nevertheless, there was a definite pattern in the evolution of instrumentalism and, like the relations between adjacent varieties of crow in the stretched genetic pool, there were connections between 'adjacent' concepts in the instrumentalist family. However, these relationships are not always obvious, particularly when the concepts concerned evolved at different times in response to widely different problems. For example, although there are philosophical and historical connections between a view of logic which suggests that the laws of deduction are to be tested by their contribution to the overall efficiency of science (concept 2) and a pragmatic theory of meaning (concept 3), and also between a pragmatic theory of meaning and the view that there is no ultimate fixed truth (concept 4), there is no obvious, direct connection between concept 2 and concept 4. If the intervening concept had not been discussed, it would have been difficult to explain why a philosopher who held a pragmatic view of the function of logic would also be likely to reject the notion of ultimate fixed truths. Consequently, the main reason for the length of the present chapter has been the need to trace these connections between apparently unrelated instrumentalist ideas, in an attempt to present a clear statement of the instrumentalist position. And the result would seem to be that there is no single instrumentalist position. One is forced to accept a variety of instrumentalist positions, because Instrumentalists rarely subscribe to all (or even most) of the concepts in the instrumentalist family.

Similarly, it appears that there are few general problems for instrumentalism, but that, as will become more evident in Chapter 3, there are often very serious problems for individual Instrumentalists. In fact, Instrumentalists have been subjected to such trenchant criticism since at least the time of Plato[141], that it seems surprising that any modern philosopher or scientist would give credence to such a philosophical attitude. But it is a fact that since 1900, Dewey, Campbell, Sullivan, Reichenbach, Toulmin, Frank, and even Nagel, to mention but a few, have espoused views of science that often appear to be instrumentalist in tone. To explain this seemingly contradictory state of affairs and to help understand instrumentalism's continuing appeal, it is necessary to look beyond its philosophical problems and examine its origins and historical development.

This matter is taken up in Chapter 3. The discussion there leads naturally to an examination of the ideas and problems of John Dewey, and hence to an examination of the relevance of instrumentalism to modern philosophy of science.

NOTES

1   Wittgenstein, L. *The Blue and Brown Books*, Blackwell, Oxford, 1969, p. 17.

2   Lovejoy, A. *The Great Chain of Being*, Harper Torch Books, N.Y., 1965, p. 3. (First published 1936.)
3   *Ibid*, p. 6.
4   Wittgenstein, *op. cit.*, p. 20.
5   *Ibid.*, p. 117.
6   Dewey, J. *The Quest for Certainty, op. cit.*, Chs 1, 2. Reichenbach, *Rise of Scientific Philosophy, op. cit.*, Chs 2, 3, 7, 8, 9.
7   Dewey, J. *Logic – The Theory of Inquiry*, Henry Holt & Co., N.Y., 1938, Chs 1–3, 19, 25. White, M. *The Age of Analysis*, Mentor Books, N.Y., 1960, p. 175. Copleston, F. *A History of Philosophy*, Vol. 8. Bellarmine Series 19, Burns & Oates Ltd, London, 1966. p. 364.
8   a. Thayer, H. *Meaning & Action*, Bobbs-Merrill Co. Ltd. N.Y., 1968 p. 85. See also Gallie's discussion of Peirce's theories.
    Gallie, W. *Peirce & Pragmatism*, Penguin, Harmondsworth, 1952 and *Philosophy & the Historical Understanding*, Schocken Books, N.Y. 1964 Ch. 7, esp. pp. 152ff. He states quite clearly that the pragmatic theory of meaning was derived from a generalising of scientific practice.
    b. Since it is difficult to describe *briefly* what is meant by a pragmatic theory of meaning, no attempt is made to do so in this short list of the characteristics of instrumentalism. For a more extensive exposition, see pp. 12ff.
9   Passmore, J. *A Hundred Years of Philosophy*, Penguin Books, 1968, p. 117; Copleston, *op. cit.*, p. 366.
10 Dewey, J. *Reconstruction in Philosophy*, Beacon Press, Boston, 1968, Introduction xxvi–xxvii, Chs 3, 7. White, *op. cit.*, p. 177.
11 Copleston, *op. cit.*, p. 354–6.
    Thayer, *op. cit.*, p. 41.
    Dewey, *Quest for Certainty, op. cit.*, ch. 5.
12 Passmore, *op. cit.*, pp. 115–6.
    Dewey, J. *Democracy & Education*, Macmillan, N.Y., 1967, pp. 272–6.
13 Dewey, *Logic – The Theory of Inquiry, op. cit.*, ch. 4.
14 Dewey, *The Quest for Certainty, op. cit.*, Ch. 7, especially pp. 184 ff.
15 *ibid.*, p. 248.
    Dewey, *Reconstruction in Philosophy, op. cit.*, pp. 61–4.
    Dewey, J. *Experience & Nature*, Dover Publications, N.Y. 1958, 2nd edition, pp. 145–6.
16 Passmore, *op. cit.*, p. 103.
    Copleston, *op. cit.*, p. 365.
    Dewey, *Quest for Certainty, op. cit.*, pp. 151–2, 157–61.
17 Dewey, *Quest for Certainty, op. cit.*, 214–16.
18 i.e. '*archetypal thinking* . . . occurs whenever a field of investigation is approached with a 'repertoire' of ideas that are being used because they proved fruitful in other investigations.'
    From Phillips, D.C. *Organicism and its influence on the Philosophical & Educational Writings of John Dewey*, Ph.D. Thesis, Melbourne University, 1968, p. 2.
    The original terminology stems from Black, M. *Models & Metaphors*, Cornell Uni. Press, N.Y., 1962, ch. 13, especially p. 241 ff, who

concentrates more on the archetype as a form of analogy than as a foundation for a philosophical system.

19 Dewey, *Logic – The Theory of Inquiry, op. cit.*, chs 1 – 3, 19, 25.

20 Dewey, *The Quest for Certainty, op. cit.*, pp. 153 – 6.

21 This view of Dewey's is discussed in some detail in both Cohen, M. *Studies in Philosophy and Science*, Frederick Ungor, N.Y., 1949. p. 149 ff and Moore, E. *American Pragmatism*, Columbia Uni. Press, N.Y., 1966, pp. 202 – 3.

22 Dewey, J. *Essays in Experimental Logic*, Dover, N.Y., p. 20.

23 e.g. Cohen, *loc. cit.*

24 e.g. his distinction between generic and universal propositions. Dewey, *Logic – The Theory of Inquiry, op. cit.*, Chs, 14, 19, esp. p. 383. For Dewey, generic propositions such as 'All Cretans are liars' refer to characteristic traits of a particular class and it is not self contradictory to assert that 'All Cretans are liars but this Cretan tells the truth', whereas universal propositions imply logical necessity and for those propositions it is self-contradictory to assert that 'All x are y but this x is a ∼ y'.

25 *Ibid.*, pp. 103 – 4.

26 Dewey, J. *Democracy and Education*, The Free Press, N.Y., 1967, pp. 219 – 20.

27 e.g. Thayer, *Meaning and Action, op. cit.*, or *The Logic of Pragmatism*, Humanities Press, N.Y. 1952.

28 e.g. see above, pp. 11 – 12.

29 Dewey, *Essays in Experimental Logic, op. cit.*, p. 84.

30 *ibid.*, p. 99.

31 Thayer, *Meaning and Action, op. cit.*, pp. x, 5.

32 See comments by Lovejoy, A. *The Thirteen Pragmatisms and Other Essays*, John Hopkins Press, Maryland, 1963, pp. 1 – 29, esp. pp. 1 – 10.

33 *ibid.*

34 Peirce, C. S. 'How to Make our Ideas Clear' in Konvitz and Kennedy, *op. cit.*, pp. 107 ff.

35 Thayer, *Meaning and Action, op. cit.*, p. 85.

36 Peirce, C. S. 'What Pragmatism Is', in *Collected papers of Charles Sanders Peirce*, Vol. 5, Harvard Uni. Press, 1960, par. 412, p. 273.

37 'Issues of Pragmatism', *Collected papers of Charles Sanders Peirce, op. cit.*, Vol. 5, par. 438, p. 293.

38 Peirce, C. S. 'How to Make our Ideas Clear' in Konvitz and Kennedy, *op. cit.*, pp. 108 ff. See also, Thayer, *Meaning and Action, op. cit.*, p. 91.

39 a. See discussion in Ayer, A. *The Origins of Pragmatism*, Macmillan, London 1968, pp. 51 – 60, 198 – 200.
b. The difficulties experienced by the pragmatists in their attempts to devise an effective theory of meaning may be compared with those of the logical positivists who put forward a similar criterion of meaning some 50 years later.

40 e.g.'Theories are only hypotheses, verified by more or less numerous facts. Those verified by most facts are the best but even then they are never final, never to be absolutely believed.' Bernard, C. *An Introduction to the Study of Experimental Medicine*, Collier, N.Y., 1961, p. 193. 'Scientific truth is that corpus of facts and provisional generalisations which, in the

consensus of competent scholars, has not yet been shown to be wrong.' Sir
Macfarlane Burnet. Quoted in Nossal, G. 'Medical Research and the
Future of Man', *University of Melbourne Gazette*, May, 1970, p. 2. 'There
are no absolutely correct assertions.' Ostwald, W. *Natural Philosophy*,
trans. Seltzer, T., Williams and Norgate, London., 1911, p. 53. See also
Frank, P. (ed) *The Validation of Scientific Theories*, Collier, N.Y., 1961,
pp. vii, 22, 74, 156, 190, and Schwab, J. 'The Structure of the Natural
Sciences' in Ford, G. and Pugno, L. *The Structure of Knowledge & the
Curriculum*, Rand McNally, Chicago, 1965, pp. 31–49, esp. pp. 33–4.

41   Passmore, *op. cit.*, p. 117. See also above pp. 10 ff.
42   Campbell, N. *Foundations of Science*, Dover, N.Y., 1957, p. 219.
43   e.g. Dewey, *Quest for Certainty, op. cit.*, Ch. 2.
44   James, W. 'Pragmatism's Conception of Truth', in Konvitz and
     Kennedy, *op. cit.*, pp. 44–61.
45   *ibid.*, pp. 51–4.
46   *ibid.*, p. 46.
47   *ibid.*, p. 53.
48   Thayer, *Meaning and Action, op. cit.*, p. 106.
49   Peirce, C. 'Mill on Induction' in *Collected Papers, op. cit.*, Vol. 2, par. 769,
     p. 491.
50   Thayer, *Meaning and Action, op. cit.*, p. 117. For a full discussion of Peirce's
     attitude, see Thayer pp. 104–20; and for a justification of Peirce's
     probability justification of induction, see Braithwaite, R. *Scientific
     Explanation*, Harper Torch Book, N.Y., 1960, pp. 264–92.
51   For Dewey, all situations were of this type. One may only know by
     interfering, by *interacting* with the environment so that both organism and
     environment are changed. See discussion of his biological model for his
     theory of knowledge, pp. 86 ff below.
52   Baker, A. *Modern Physics and Antiphysics*, Addison-Wesley, London, 1970,
     Ch. 16 *passim*, pp. 219–21.
53   Copleston, *op. cit.*, pp. 306, 379; White, *op. cit.*, pp. 157–8.
54   Passmore, *op. cit.*, p. 112.
55   White, *op. cit.*, p. 159.
56   Passmore, *op. cit.*, p. 117.
57   Campbell, *op. cit.*, pp. 215, 219; Copleston, *op. cit.*, p. 337. Ziman,
     J. *Public Knowledge*, Cambridge University Press, 1968, *passim*.
58   Copleston, *op. cit.*, p. 366; Macfarlane Burnet, in Nossal, G. *loc. cit*; Ziman,
     op. cit., passim.
59   See discussion in Braithwaite, *op. cit.*, p. 264 ff.
60   e.g. it was in this general area that G. E. Moore launched his famous
     attack on pragmatism in 1922. See Moore, G. E. *Philosophical Studies*,
     London, Routledge and Kegan Paul, 1922, ch. 3.
61   e.g. the traditional problem of drawing a boundary between Reason and
     Faith. See Aquinas, Descartes, Kant, Spinoza etc.
62   Dewey, J. *Experience & Nature*, Dover, N.Y., 1958; *The Quest for Certainty*,
     Capricorn Books, N.Y., 1960; *Reconstruction in Philosophy*, Beacon Press.
     Boston, 1968; *Problems of Men*, Philosophy Library, N.Y., 1946, esp. part
     2, section 4; and numerous other essays and articles.

63   Reichenbach, *Rise of Scientific Philosophy, op. cit.*
64   Dewey, *Reconstruction in Philosophy, op. cit.*, pp. ix.
65   Dewey, *Quest for Certainty, op. cit.*, pp. 258–68; *Problems of Men, op. cit.*, part III, sect. 1. For a full discussion of Dewey's ideas about ethics and values, see Thayer, *Meaning & Action, op. cit.*, pp. 393–414.
66   Dewey, *Quest for Certainty, op. cit.*, p. 259.
67   Dewey, *Reconstruction in Philosophy, op. cit.*, p. 169.
68   McCloskey, H.'An Examination of Restricted Utilitarianism' and 'A Non Utilitarian Approach to Punishment' in Bayles, M. *Contemporary Utilitarianism*, Anchor Books, N.Y., 1968, pp. 117–42, 239–60.
69   Warnock, G. *Contemporary Moral Philosophy*, Macmillan, London, 1967.
70   See above, pp. 4, 10, 11–12.
71   Passmore, *op. cit.*, p. 115.
72   Copleston, *op. cit.*, pp. 353, 357.
73   Passmore, *op. cit.*, pp. 115, 117.
74   Dewey, *Democracy & Education, op. cit.*, p. 344.
75   See his discussion of anthropocentrism: 'The history of science, indeed, may be considered as a chronicle of the painful decrease in humanity's sense of its central role in the universe . . .' McLaughlin, R. *Theoretical Entities & Philosophical Dualisms*, Ph.D. thesis, Indiana University, 1967, p. 239 ff.
76   Passmore, *op. cit.*, p. 116; Copleston, *op. cit.*, pp. 354–5.
77   Dewey, J. *How We Think*, Heath & Co, Boston, 1933, p. 105.
78   *ibid.*, Chs 5–7. This scheme is in many ways similar to the chemist Ostwald's description of scientific method, see Ostwald, W. *Natural Philosophy*, Williams & Norgate, London, 1911, pp. 43 ff. It also agrees to a considerable extent with Schwab's modified form for scientific inquiry. See Schwab, J. 'The Structure of Disciplines: Meaning and Significances' in Ford & Pugno, *op. cit.*, pp. 6–30.
79   c.f. Toulmin's comments re analogy between theories and maps in Toulmin, S. *Philosophy of Science*, Hutchinson, London, 1953, Chapter 4.
80   Dewey, *How We Think, op. cit.*, p. 115.
81   *ibid.*, p. 116.
82   *ibid.*, p. 12.
83   My insertion.
84   Dewey, *How We Think, op. cit.*, p. 73.
85   *ibid.*, p. 74.
86   Popper, K. *The Logic of Scientific Discovery*, Hutchinson, London, 1959, pp. 31 ff.
87   Reichenbach, *op. cit.*, pp. 231 ff.
88   e.g. Margenau, H. *et al*, *Physics*, McGraw-Hill, N.Y., 1950.
89   Harvey, W. *The Circulation of the Blood & Other Writings*, London, 1952.
90   Darwin, C. *On the Origin of the Species by Means of Natural Selection*, New. American Library (Mentor M Q 503), 1964.
91   i.e. pp. 19–22.
92   e.g. See Dewey, *Logic – The Theory of Inquiry, op. cit.*, pp. 427, 432, 484–5; and Peirce, C. 'The Logic of Abduction' in *Essays in the Philosophy of Science*, Bobbs-Merrill, N.Y., 1957, pp. 237. See also discussions in Popper,

Logic of Scientific Discovery, op. cit., pp. 31 ff. and Reichenbach, *Rise of Scientific Philosophy, op. cit.*, pp. 231 ff.

93 Dewey, *Quest for Certainty*, pp. 153–6.

94 This claim was discussed above, pp. 11–13.

95 Dewey, *Quest for Certainty, op. cit.*, p. 138.

96 For a comprehensive discussion of Dewey's position see Thayer, *Meaning and Action, op. cit.*, pp. 165 f and 190 f. I shall return to this topic in Chapter 4.

97 Dewey, *Quest for Certainty, op. cit.*, pp. 155.

98 Copleston, *op. cit.*, p. 356.

99 For a detailed discussion of this opinion see Thayer, *Meaning and Action, op. cit.*, p. 41 ff.

100 Reichenbach, *op. cit.*, chs 11, 14, 16. See also discussions in Nagel, E. *The Structure of Science*, Routledge and Kegal Paul, London, 1961, p. 137 ff. The argument runs roughly as follows: The fact that theories have indispensable functions in inquiry does not preclude them from also being regarded as 'genuine statements' whose 'truth' or 'falsity' may be investigated when appropriate.

101 Dewey,*Quest for Certainty, op. cit.*, pp. 67–70, 192 ff. See also Passmore, *op. cit.*, pp. 115–6.

102 Dewey, *Logic – The Theory of Inquiry, op. cit.*, Ch. 4.

103 e.g. Dewey, *Logic – The Theory of Inquiry, passim* and *Quest for Certainty, passim*.

104 Dewey, *The Quest for Certainty*, pp. 172–3.

105 Bernard, *op. cit.*, Ch. V and esp. pp. 193–5.

106 This topic was more fully discussed above re Peirce's views of truth, pp. 15–16.

107 c.f. Dewey's remarks about some methods of inquiry being better than others. See *Logic – The Theory of Inquiry*, pp. 104.

108 Dewey, *Logic – The Theory of Inquiry, op. cit.*, pp. 8–9 and Ch. VII. For a discussion of the problems associated with this approach, see Thayer, *Meaning and Action, op. cit.*, pp. 193 ff.

109 Harré, R. (ed) *Scientific Thought 1900–1960*, Clarendon Press, Oxford, 1969, pp. 18–34; Dewey, *Quest for Certainty, op. cit.*, pp. 142–6.

110 5600 seconds of arc instead of 5557 seconds of arc per century.

111 i.e. that the Lorentz equations, $x' = B(x-vt)$, $t' = B(t-\frac{vx}{c^2})$,

$B = (1-\frac{v^2}{c^2})^{-\frac{1}{2}}$, reduce to the Newtonian equations, $x' = x-vt$ and $t' = t$

when (v) is much smaller than (c).

112 Dewey, *Quest for Certainty, op. cit.*, pp. 83–4.

113 *ibid.*, pp. 146–7.

114 c.f. example given by Dewey, *Quest for Certainty, op. cit.*, pp. 173–4.

115 e.g. see Peirce, C. 'The Fixation of Belief' in *Collected Papers, op. cit.*, Vol. 5, par. 358–87 (esp. par. 384), pp. 223–47.

116 Dewey, *Quest for Certainty, op. cit.*, p. 241.

117 See discussion in Thayer, *Meaning and Action, op. cit.*, Part II, Chs 1 and 3.

118 Margenau, H. et al, *op. cit.*, Ch 20.
119 *ibid.*, p. 704.
120 *ibid.*, p. 697.
121 Danto, A. and Morgenbesser, G. *Philosophy of Science*, Meridian Books, N. Y., 1960, pp. 459–61.
122 Nagel, E. *op. cit.*, pp. 160–2.
123 See discussion below, Chapters 3 and 4.
124 Dewey, *The Quest for Certainty*, op. cit., pp. 151–2, 157–61, 216–8.
125 *ibid.*, pp. 218–9.
126 Dewey, *Quest for Certainty, op. cit.* pp. 206–7, 248, *Experience and Nature*, Dover, N.Y., 1958, p. 148; Passmore, *op. cit.*, p. 103.
127 Toulmin, *Philosophy of Science, op. cit.*, pp. 79 ff.
128 See the works of Mach, Pearson, Poincaré, Duhem, and Ostwald cited in the bibliography. For further discussion, see Chapter 3 below.
129 Copleston, *op. cit.*, p. 365; Dewey, *Logic: The Theory of Inquiry, op. cit.*, ch 22.
130 See discussion of Truth, pp. 15–18.
131 See discussions of Thinking, pp. 19–22, Science, pp. 23–4, Relations, pp. 24–6.
132 Thayer, *Meaning and Action, op. cit.*, p. 116.
133 Peirce, C. S. 'The Fixation of Belief', *Collected Papers of Charles Sanders Peirce, op. cit.*, Vol. 5, p. 366.
134 Farrington, B. *Greek Science*, Pelican, 1944, pp. 127, 129.
135 For instance, see above, pp. 11–13, on Dewey's ideas about the *development* of logic.
136 For a detailed exposition of each concept see pp. 10–11 above.
137 Lovejoy, *The Thirteen Pragmatisms, op. cit.*, p. 35.
138 See above, pp. 10–11.
139 See Chapter 3 for details. As an example of the issues involved, see Meyerson's comments concerning Leibniz's and Huygen's discussions about whether elementary particles should be considered as infinitely elastic or as infinitely hard. Meyerson, E. *Identity & Reality*, Dover, 1962, pp. 407 ff. See also Peirce's comments about the views of the 'older generation' of physicists. Peirce, C. *Essays in the Philosophy of Science*, N.Y. 1957, pp. 161–2.
140 For discussion of these matters see Chapters 3, 4, 5.
141 See discussion above, Chapter 1 and this chapter.

3
The Development of the Instrumentalist Family of Concepts before Dewey

> It seems that the search for certainty can make a man blind to the postulates of logic, that the attempt to base knowledge on reason alone can make him abandon the principles of cogent reasoning.[1]

As was suggested at the end of Chapter 2, a brief examination of the historical antecedents of instrumentalism serves two main purposes. That is, it helps to explain—

1 why philosophical difficulties have not been fatal to the instrumentalist view of science and
2 why the modern instrumentalist family of concepts contains those elements discussed in Chapter 2.

Ideas are not bred in isolation, and philosophers have long found it useful to begin a discussion of their own ideas by tracing the development of similar or contrary concepts in previous literature. Plato and Aristotle regularly used this technique, as have many recent innovators in philosophy. The reason for this predilection among philosophers for introducing their own work by means of a discussion of the work of their predecessors is straightforward. It is much easier to explain what is new when it is presented against the background from which it grew. As Bronowski notes when discussing Newton,

> To see what happened about 1660, we must look at the landscape of science and thought before that time, and see what it looked like before the change quickened it.[2]

Much the same may be said of instrumentalism; to understand what happened in the philosophy of science in the early years of the present century, it is essential to examine the landscape of science and philosophy before that time.

A similar thesis is expressed by Lovejoy, when he suggests—

> . . . that the working of a given conception, of an explicit or tacit pre-

supposition, of a type of mental habit, or of a specific thesis or argument, needs, if its *nature* and its historic role are to be *fully* understood, to be traced connectedly through all the phases of men's reflective life in which those workings manifest themselves, or through as many of them as the historian's resources permit.[3]

A further consideration which is more relevant to purpose 1 than to purpose 2 is illustrated by Lovejoy, when he says that—

> . . . a formulated doctrine is sometimes a relatively inert thing. The conclusion reached by a process of thought is also not infrequently the conclusion of the process of thought. The more significant factor in the matter may be, not the dogma which certain persons proclaim—be that simple or manifold in its meaning—but the motives or reasons which have led them to it.[4]

As Boring points out, this pursuit of 'motives or reasons' frequently leads us outside philosophy to consider the 'zeitgeist', or current culture and climate of opinion, as they affect thinking. Such excursions are not digressions, they are necessary prerequisites to an understanding of changes in philosophic and scientific theories.[5]

Instrumentalism in Philosophical Thought

Like most philosophical attitudes, modern instrumentalism grew out of a dissatisfaction with contemporary ideas. During much of the latter half of the nineteenth century, scientists and philosophers were constantly questioning the adequacy of traditional ideas about the status of 'theoretical entities' (such as electro-magnetic fields), about the standing of scientific laws, and about the appropriateness of the mechanistic model then used in science. The resulting discussions led to a re-appraisal of much of philosophy of science, and became part of the more general upheaval in philosophy which later produced pragmatism, utilitarianism, and an emphasis on what has since been termed linguistic philosophy.

Instrumentalism is derived from pragmatism, and may even be regarded as a form of pragmatism.[6] Consequently, any attempt to trace the development of the main instrumentalist concepts involves an excursion deep into history, because pragmatists claim for their philosophy the most ancient of antecedents. To paraphrase William James, Instrumentalism is a new name for an old way of thinking, and he, Peirce, and Dewey were all very conscious of the influence of both ancient and contemporary ideas on their own theories. As a result, they would frequently introduce a new topic by referring to the writings of the Greek philosophers, or by discussing the views of some of the nineteenth-century thinkers. James, in particular, was concerned that his pragmatic approach be seen as part of the mainstream of philosophy. In 'What Pragmatism Means', he maintained that, 'pragmatism . . . being nothing essentially new, harmonizes with many ancient philosophic tendencies. It agrees with nominalism . . . with utilitarianism . . . with positivism . . . ',[7] and he constantly asserted that pragmatism represented a perfectly familiar attitude to philosophy, the empiricist attitude.[8] To support this view, he cited Socrates, Aristotle, Locke, Berkeley, and Hume, as previous practitioners of the pragmatic method.[9] He also put forward the ideas of Sigwart, Mach, Ostwald, Pearson, Milhaud, Poincaré, Duhem, and Ruyssen as the basis from which he had developed his own philosophy.[10] Furthermore, he was quite confident that Dewey and he were simply following the example of successful scientists.[11] Peirce, too, emphasised the way ideas were influenced by the zeitgeist. For example, in 'The Fixation of Belief', Section 1, while congratulating Kepler on a marvellous piece of inductive reasoning, Peirce noted that Kepler's methods, like those of every worker in science, had suffered to a certain extent from some exemplification of the defective state of reasoning of the time when it was written.[12] As well, like James, Peirce often introduced his own ideas by reference to, and discussion of, the ideas of scientist/philosophers such as Poincaré, Pearson, and Mach.[13]

Dewey accepted a similar point of view and, while using the past to demonstrate the origin of an idea or its faults (or both),[14] stressed the thesis that the problems of philosophy have always grown from the intellectual and moral issues of their own time and place.[15]

Whether one fully accepts Dewey's thesis or not, it would seem that an understanding of the historical development of the instrumentalist family of ideas is useful, and perhaps necessary, to an understanding of the persistent role of the instrumentalist attitude in philosophy of science. However, before turning to an examination of the intellectual zeitgeist of the late nineteenth century, it is advantageous to briefly re-capitulate, and make plain which beliefs are to be treated as the most commonly accepted elements of instrumentalism. The instrumentalist 'family' revolves around the suggestion that science is the result of man's interaction with his environment (including his attempts to control that environment), and is usually characterised by a belief in—

1   the suggestion that logic is a description of those methods of inquiry that are successful,
2   a pragmatic theory of meaning,
3   the suggestion that there are no ultimate, fixed truths in science,
4   the compatibility of science and ethics,
5   a view of thought which sees ideas as intellectual tools and guides to practice,
6   the theory that knowledge is the formulation of successful

practice,

7   the suggestion that science is a complex form of the process of inquiry,

8   the view that scientific theories are never absolute,

9   the notion that relations rather than events are the basis of science,

10   the suggestion that scientific laws are more akin to statistical regularities than to mechanical rules,

11   the assumption that method is more important than subject matter.

Instrumentalism in Ancient Thought

What is now known as instrumentalism has always been something of a scientist's philosophy of science, and instrumentalist doctrines have usually been derived from contemporary scientific practice. Consequently, particularly in recent times, much of the criticism of instrumentalism by philosophers has been 'wasted' on other philosophers, and has had little or no impact on the opinions of scientists who, in the course of their work, have very often found it convenient to think in instrumentalist terms.[16]

This association of an instrumentalist mode of thought with contemporary scientific practices developed very early in the history of science, and, as a result, it is appropriate to turn first, as did Peirce, Dewey, and Reichenbach, to a study of the writings of the Ancient Greek scientists.

Now, 'Greek thinking' like 'instrumentalism' was not one unified mode of thought, and the Greek archetype went through a series of changes. In fact, 'Greek thought' was as varied as 'Modern English thought', and suffered from the same series of divisions; due sometimes to disputes about evidence and reasoning, but often to intellectual fads, fashions, and fancies. One of these 'fads' was an approach to science which was similar to instrumentalism and which appeared to have become popular about 500 B.C., particularly in the writings of those Greeks who were concerned mainly with medical matters.

Between 600 and 800 B.C., there developed in Greece an important new class of merchants and manufacturers who instituted new ways of thinking and began to re-organise science. The working lives of these men were mainly concerned with tools and techniques, and their way of thinking was strongly influenced by 'methods' and 'use'. Perhaps most important of all, their lives revolved around a system of trade and currency which was derived from Mesopotamia, and which involved methods of calculation and ways of thinking that were concerned with practical utility and with controlling the environment to return a profit.

By the fifth century B.C., there is little doubt that the Greeks were beginning to equate the improvement of methods with the growth of intelligence. Aeschylus (circa 460 B.C.) suggested that primitive man could be likened to a baby who knows nothing and must learn everything,[17] and that as he developed, man measured his development by what he could do—the homes he could build, the calendar he had devised, the calculations he could make, the plants he could grow, the animals he could use, the illness he could cure, and so on. Sophocles[18] (circa 440 B.C.) saw man as the pinnacle of creation, because he forced nature to help him. That is, it was man's technical ingenuity which demonstrated his wisdom. Anaxagoras[19] believed that man became wise because he possessed hands which might be used in an infinitude of ways. In fact, the empiricist school of pre-Platonic Greek science constantly stressed that what was important was methods; results were transitory, what mattered was the successful method which would consistently produce the desired results. For instance, Celsus, writing at the beginning of the first century A.D., said of the 'Empirici' (e.g. Serapion, Apollonius, Glaucias, Heraclides):

On the other hand, those who take the name of Empirici from their experience do indeed accept evident causes as necessary; but they contend that inquiry about obscure causes and natural actions is superfluous, because nature is not to be comprehended. That nature cannot be comprehended is in fact patent, they say, from the disagreement among those who discuss such matters; for on this question there is no agreement either among professors of philosophy or among actual medical practicioners. Since, therefore, the cause is as uncertain as it is incomprehensible, protection is to be sought rather from the ascertained and explored, as in all the rest of the Arts, that is, from what experience has taught in the actual course of treatment: for even a farmer, or a pilot, is made not by disputation but by practice. That such speculations[20] are not pertinent to the Art of Medicine may be learned from the fact that men may hold different opinions on these matters, yet conduct their patients to recovery all the same. This has happened, not because they deduced lines of healing from obscure causes, nor from the natural actions, concerning which different opinions were held, but from experiences of what had previously succeeded. Even in its beginnings, they add, the Art of Medicine was not deduced from such questionings, but from experience; for of the sick who were without doctors, some in the first days of illness, longing for food, took it forthwith; others, owing to distaste, abstained; and the illness was more alleviated in those who abstained. Again, some partook of food whilst actually under the fever, some a little before, others after its remission, and it went best with those who did so after the fever had ended; and similarly some at the beginning adopted at once a rather full diet, others a scanty one, and those were made worse who had eaten plentifully. When this and the like happened day after day, careful men noted what generally answered for better, and then began to prescribe the same for their patients.

Thus sprang up the Art of Medicine, which, from the frequent recovery of some and the death of others, distinguished between the pernicious and the salutary.[21]

Furthermore, the early Greek thinkers realised that many of nature's processes take place in such a way that they cannot be directly observed. Consequently, they believed that these hidden relations could only be explained by inference from observed operations. For example, the writings of the Hippocratic School of Medicine amply demonstrate that these ancient doctors realised that much happened within the body which could be explained or at least predicted by reasoning based on careful observations of the body's external reactions.

> Without doubt no man who sees only with his eyes can know anything of what has been here described. It is for this reason that I have called them obscure even as they have been judged to be by the art. Their obscurity, however, does not mean that they are our masters, but as far as is possible they have been mastered, a possibility limited only by the capacity of the sick to be examined and of researchers to conduct research. More pains, in fact, and quite as much time, are required to know them as if they were seen with the eyes; for what escapes the eyesight is mastered by the eye of the mind, and the sufferings of patients due to their not being quickly observed are the fault, not of the medical attendants, but of the nature of the patient and of the disease. The attendant in fact, as he could neither see the trouble with his eyes nor learn it with his ears, tried to track it by reasoning.[22]

> Now medicine, being prevented, in cases of empyema, and of diseased liver, kidneys, and the cavities generally, from seeing with the sight with which all men see everything most perfectly, has never-the-less discovered other means to help it. There is clearness or roughness of the voice, rapidity or slowness of respiration, and for the customary discharges the ways through which they severally pass, sometimes smell, sometimes colour, sometimes thinness or thickness furnishing medicine with the means of inferring what condition these symptoms indicate, what symptoms mean that a part is already affected and what that a part may hereafter be affected.[23]

They also believed that practical circumstances *forced* men to develop medicine, because the sick do not benefit from the same treatment as do the healthy. As a result, the precursor of the doctor was an artisan, the cook, because it was he who took the raw foods of nature and treated them so that man might easily assimmilate them and gain maximum benefit from his eating.[24] They spoke of 'practioners of the art', and referred to themselves as craftsmen.[25] Clearly, it was methods and results which these men saw as important.

In fact, shades of the history of controversy between extreme Instrumentalists and Realists are suggested when one of the Hippocratic writers scolds the followers of Empedocles for suggesting that the science of medicine could be based on 'postulates' such as the theory of the four elements (earth, air, fire, and water) rather than practice.[26] The ancient doctor's objections are instructive. He opposes 'postulates' because they cannot be checked or verified, because there is no way of applying them. He opposed the suggestion that there can be only a few basic postulates, because he could not see how a practising doctor could accept a very limited range of causes for disease. He suggested that, not only were the philosophers wrong, but they were 'especially to be blamed' because they were wrong about an art. That is, were wrong about something that was based on practice, where the 'wrong' does not belong because it would not work in practice, and hence would soon be discarded. Finally, he objected because medicine was a particular *kind* of art, that is, because of the importance of medicine to mankind; an importance which it had gained because men have recourse to the art of Healing at the crises of life, 'and give the greatest honours to the good craftsmen and practitioners in it',[27] to those who consistently cure their patients.

The instrumentalist emphasis is plain; *successful* practice rather than fine theories was what the physician should strive for.

> Wherefore I have deemed that it has no need of an empty postulate, as do insoluble mysteries, about which any exponent must use a postulate, for example, things in the sky or below the earth. If a man were to learn and declare the state of these, neither to the speaker himself nor to his audience would it be clear whether his statements were true or not. For there is no test the application of which would give certainty. But medicine has long had all its means to hand, and has discovered both a principle and a method, through which the discoveries made during a long period are many and excellent, while full discovery will be made, if the inquirer be competent, conduct his researches with knowledge of the discoveries already made, and make them his starting-point. But anyone who, casting aside and rejecting all these means, attempts to conduct research in any other way or after another fashion, and asserts that he has found out anything, is and has been the victim of deception.[28]

Now, it might be objected that this emphasis on method is not peculiar to instrumentalism, and that almost any philosophical creed would be compatible with the claims of Celsus and the members of the Hippocratic school. And with this objection the writer would agree. However, it is not claimed that a preference for practice is unique to instrumentalism. The claim made in Chapter 2 was a much weaker one—that such an emphasis on method is commonly supported by philosophers who are usually accepted as Instrumentalists (e.g. Dewey) and, for that reason, has been put forward as a member of the instrumentalist family of concepts. As well, this point serves to emphasise the claim made by James in 'What Pragmatism Means' and discussed earlier in this book, that the Instrumentalist, the Realist, the Idealist, and the Empiricist have much in common, and therefore that it is quite possible for an Instrumentalist to hold similar ideas to, say, a Realist, in some fields, and vice versa. Few, if any, of the concepts in the instrumentalist family belong to instrumentalism alone.

Before leaving the writings of the Hippocratic school, one final point should be made. Namely, that throughout *On Ancient Medicine* and *The Art*, the emphasis was constantly on experience combined with reason as the basis of medicine. That is, there was a clear attempt to see man always in relation to his environment. This theme also occurred in *Airs, Waters and Places*,[29] where the physician explained that man is affected by the climate, by the food he eats, the waters he drinks, and so on, and was again emphasised in *Regimen on Acute Diseases*.[30]

This basically instrumentalist type of approach was not typical of all of Greek science however, and contrasted strongly with the more a priori methods of the cosmologist. For instance, Plato in the *Timaeus* suggested that only the simple minded would suppose that the evidence provided by the eye would give good grounds for reasoning about the things in the heavens.[31] Aristotle, although often critical of Plato and his theories, was cast in a similar mould. There is no doubt that his biological writings give ample evidence of extensive and detailed observations, but the reader is always conscious of the metaphysical assumptions which continually intruded when explanations were being offered.[32] And, when he moved from biology to sciences with which he was less familiar (e.g. physics) it was soon evident that metaphysics had become more important than observation. For example, the Aristotelean explanation of movement was based on the idea of 'natural places' for each of the four basic elements, and suggested that the atmosphere was both the resistor and promulgator of motion.[33] Although this theory was obviously unsatisfactory when applied to projectile motion, it was not discarded even though it ran counter to observation.

Aristotle's cosmology was even less observation-orientated. Here his basic postulate was that the heavens are eternal, incorruptible, and unchanging, while the earth is finite, corruptible, and forever undergoing change.[34] Therefore the shape appropriate to these 'perfect' heavens was the 'perfect' shape, the circle, and the appropriate motion was uniform circular motion because such motion has no change, no beginning, no end, and is thus 'perfect'. These non-empirical arguments were supported by a certain amount of common-sense knowledge about nature, but, generally, his approach was anti-instrumentalist in tone.

For well-known historical, social, and intellectual reasons, the Platonic and Aristotelean systems dominated European thought from about 350 B.C. to the seventeenth century,[35] but the instrumentalist point of view was not entirely lost, and isolated examples of instrumentalist thinking appeared at various times, particularly after 1400 A.D. Agricola[36] (circa 1430) in *De Re Metallica* treated matter as something to be manipulated to produce the results desired by man, and paid only lip service to the prevailing theories of matter which were still Greek in essence and were not very useful to the miner.

In fact, at that stage the 'science' of Alchemy and the magic and myths associated with it was in the process of being rejected by society because the alchemists had not been successful and, after some ten centuries, had failed to produce techniques that would transmute base metals into those that were more precious.

Another example was the work of the physician, Vesalius (circa 1545).[37] He also tended to reject metaphysical postulates and arguments from authority as the basis for science, and argued for a return to observation as the starting point for the development of theories about nature. As a result, although Vesalius knew full well that he risked the ridicule of his fellow academics, he claimed that the natural order in the human body could only be apprehended by the evidence provided by the senses, and that if the evidence of his (Vesalius') dissections disagreed with traditional teachings, then those teachings were wrong.[38]

Finally there are the writings of Francis Bacon[39] (circa 1600), who suggested that what is most useful in practice is most correct in theory, that in nature practical results are the guarantee of truth,[40] and that valuable lessons for philosophy may be derived from the methods of the mechanical arts.[41]

Instrumentalism in Modern Thought

Despite the influence of men such as Agricola, Vesalius, and Bacon, instrumentalism did not again become an important ingredient in scientific thinking until the last half of the nineteenth and the early years of the twentieth century. At this stage, the idea that the best scientific theories are those that allow man to manipulate his environment most successfully and predict the future behaviour of his variables most accurately was once more becoming popular among practising scientists, and the initial stimulus for a revival of instrumentalism came mainly from men such as Helmholtz, Bernard, Stallo, Boltzmann, Pearson, Hertz, Peirce, James, Mach, Poincaré, Ostwald, Duhem, and Meyerson, who were not only active in science or mathematics but were also writing about the philosophical bases of their disciplines. However, their views met considerable opposition and, in reacting to criticism, their natural instrumentalist leanings often tended to lead them to exaggerate their position. In particular, although few of these writers specifically deny the possibility that man could eventually come to know the essential essence of things, the difficulty of demonstrating the 'real' existence of an atom, or an electron, or an electro-magnetic field (etc.) at that stage in scientific development appeared to cause an unnecessarily heavy emphasis by writers with instrumentalist leanings on the purely utilitarian nature of scientific theories. However, they had some justification for their position because, although theoretical entities like electrons might be difficult to explain in traditional terms, these men had behind them nearly two hundred years of intense and highly successful scientific practice based on the Newtonian framework, and they often seemed to believe that it mattered little whether their unobservables had 'real' existence or not, because their theories worked and worked well.

Consequently, there is some justification for one of the more common criticisms of instrumentalism, i.e., that the instrumentalist position leads to a denial of the possibility of the 'existence' of theoretical entities.[42] Certainly Ostwald (often) and Dewey (sometimes) held that the essence of things cannot be known by man. However, most Instrumentalists left the position open, and asserted neither the existence nor non-existence of their theoretical terms. As Nagel[43] points out, it is clearly not logically inconsistent to discuss the existence of atoms and electrons on the one hand, and also recognise the important instrumental function of theories on the other. As a result, Instrumentalists felt free to choose whichever interpretation of theoretical terms best suited their needs and, naturally enough, produced a variety of different accounts of the various 'scientific objects' postulated by scientific theories. Be that as it may, there is little doubt that instrumentalist concepts were increasingly emphasised by scientists and philosophers in the last half of the nineteenth century.

One of the first writers to demonstrate this new tendency towards an instrumentalist mode of thought was Hermann Helmholtz (circa 1860), who attacked Kant's beliefs about the origins of geometry. Although he agreed with Kant that knowledge involved both empirical and non empirical elements, he was not willing to accept Kant's view that geometrical axioms were examples of a priori intuitions, and was concerned to demonstrate that they were the products of experience.

> In conclusion, I would again urge that the axioms of geometry are not propositions pertaining only to the pure doctrine of space. As I said before, they are concerned with quantity. We can speak of quantities only when we know of some way by which we can compare, divide, and measure them. All space-measurements, and therefore in general all ideas of quantities applied to space, assume the possibility of figures moving without change of form or

size. It is true we are accustomed in geometry to call such figures purely geometrical solids, surfaces, angles, and lines, because we abstract from all the other distinctions, physical and chemical, of natural bodies; but yet one physical quality, rigidity, is retained. Now we have no other mark of rigidity of bodies or figures but congruence, whenever they are applied to one another at any time or place, and after any revolution. We cannot, however, decide by pure geometry, and without mechanical considerations, whether the coinciding bodies may not both have varied in the same sense.[44]

Thus the axioms of geometry are not concerned with space relations only but also at the same time with the mechanical deportment of solid bodies in motion.[45]

This emphasis on experience as the primary basis of knowledge became endemic in science in the eighteen sixties, and the doctor/biologist, Claude Bernard, (circa 1866) was another very fluent and influential writer on the subject. He considered that there were two main starting points for scientific research, (*a*) observations and (*b*) hypotheses or theories.[46] In each case his emphasis was on facts and observations, which might be considered analogous to the fixed pylons on which a bridge is built. Theories and hypotheses were also essential, but they were not fixed and immutable. They were analogous to the spans between the pylons. That is, they connect the pylons and are essential to complete the bridge but, at any stage, might be lifted and replaced by another span of different and 'better' design.[47]

Here Bernard was illustrating one of the more common instrumentalist notions—that a theory is an instrument in a technique for inferring observation statements from other such statements.[48] In most other respects, also, his views about the role of scientific theories were instrumentalist in tone. For example, with regard to the form of research initiated by observation (type (*a*)), Bernard suggested that —

When we see a phenomenon which we are not in the habit of seeing, we must always ask ourselves what it is connected with, or putting it differently, what is its proximate cause; the answer or idea which presents itself to the mind, must then be submitted to experiment.[49]

. . . we see how chance observation of a fact or phenomenon brings to birth, by anticipation, a preconceived idea or hypothesis about the probable cause of the phenomenon observed; how the preconceived idea begets reasoning which results in the experiment which verifies it; how in one case, we had to have recourse to experimentation, i.e. to the use of more or less complicated operative processes, etc., to work out the verification. In the last example, experiment played a double role; it first judged and confirmed the provisions of the reasoning which it had begotten; but what is more, it produced a fresh observation. We may therefore call this observation an observation produced or begotten by experiment. This proves that, as we said, all the results of an experiment must be observed, both those connected with the preconceived idea and those without any relation to it. If we saw only facts connected with our preconceived idea, we should often cut ourselves off from making discoveries. For it often happens that an unsuccessful experiment may produce an excellent observation . . .[50]

However, despite his heavy emphasis on fact, observation, and experiments, Bernard did not denigrate theories and hypotheses. They had their place, a very important place, because they were useful. For instance, when commenting on research initiated by hypothesis (type (*b*)), Bernard observed that—

> We have already said and we shall see further on, that in noting an observation we must never go beyond facts. But in making an experiment, it is different. I wish to show that hypotheses are indispensable, and that they are useful, therefore, precisely because they lead us outside of facts and carry science forward. The object of hypotheses is not only to make us try new experiments; they also often make us discover new facts which we should not have perceived without them.[51]

On the other hand, he was careful to note that no scientist should ever have complete confidence in any theory, no matter how well supported it may be, because—

1   he may then ignore or overlook facts which are contrary to the theory, and
2   facts are the foundation of science, while theories are only hypotheses which often have to be revised or replaced.

> . . . So I noted a new fact, unforeseen in theory, which men had not noticed, doubtless because they were under the influence of contrary theories which they had too confidently accepted. I therefore abandoned my hypothesis on the spot . . .
>   In these researches I followed the principles of the experimental method that we have established, i.e., that, in the presence of a well-noted, new fact which contradicts a theory, instead of keeping the theory and abandoning the fact, I should keep and study the fact, and I hastened to give up the theory, thus conforming to the precept which we proposed in the second chapter: 'When we meet a fact which contradicts a prevailing theory, we must accept the fact and abandon the theory, even when the theory is supported by great names and generally accepted.
>   We must therefore distinguish, as we said, between principles and theories, and never believe absolutely in the latter . . .'[52]

To sum up, theories are only hypotheses, verified by more or less numerous facts. Those verified by the most facts are the best; but even then they are never final, never to be absolutely believed. We have seen in the preceding examples that if we had had complete confidence in the prevailing theory of the destruction of sugar in animals, and if we had only had its confirmation in view, we should probably not have found the road to the new facts which we met. It is true that a hypothesis based on a theory produced the experiment; but as soon as the results of the experiment appeared, theory and hypothesis had to disappear, for the experimental facts were now just an observation, to be made without any preconceived idea.[53]

Although his emphasis on the tentative status of scientific theories is strongly instrumentalist in tone, there was little in Bernard's approach that would offend the philosophical sensibilities of a modern 'Realist'. However, Johann Stallo (circa 1880) in his attack on contemporary simplistic mechanistic theories (which tended to suggest that the elementary particles of matter were simple, similar, inert, absolutely hard, and perfectly elastic) carried the instrumentalist approach to its extreme, rejecting the 'reality' of atoms and suggesting that hypotheses may involve fictitious assumptions.[54]

And the futility of such hypotheses goes to the verge of mischievous puerility when they replace a single fact by a number of arbitrary assumptions, among which is the fact itself. Some of the uses made of the atomic hypothesis, both in physics and chemistry, which have been discussed in the last chapter, afford conspicuous examples of this class of bootless assumptions; and similar instances abound among the mathematical formulae that are not infrequently paraded as physical theories.[55]

An hypothesis may involve not only one but several fictitious assumptions, provided they bring into relief, or point to the probability, or at least possibility, of an agreement between phenomena in a particular that is real and observable.[56]

His extreme position was not accepted by many scientists, however, and even those who favoured his rejection of the mechanistic philosophy of science found it difficult to draw the line at what was real and not real, observable and non-observable.[57] For instance, was a small crystal a large molecule; and do bacteria exist, even though they may only be seen through a powerful microscope? Such questions make it plain that the setting up of an observable/non-observable distinction in science will inevitably lead to problems. In fact, there is still considerable controversy about this matter in modern literature,[58] and the difficulties involved will be discussed in chapters 4 and 5, when Dewey's ideas about the status of 'physical' objects (the objects of physics) are considered.

Another anti-mechanist approach (but one which was much more in keeping with the growing instrumentalist attitude to science) was that of the philosopher Emile Boutroux (circa 1880). He taught that—

> The distinction between laws or relations and phenomena or elements, copied from that between precepts and will, is a mental artifice for the reduction to ideas of the greatest possible amount of given reality. In being itself, this distinction disappears, and with it the determinism which implies it.[59]

His basic thesis was always that the concept of determinism arose from the way men connect things to make them intelligible, and that natural science only teaches us the means of influencing and governing nature. He also claimed that it was by a process of artificial construction and abstraction that we isolate a world of atoms and mechanical forces.[60] However, he did not mean to imply that mechanical laws were fictitious because, although the concept of a law is the result of the effort man makes to adapt things to the mind and make them intelligible, such laws are not purely mental constructs but result from the collaboration of mind and things.[61] He did not want to accept complete necessity in natural science, but admitted that—

> In things, there is a mode of being which suggests to our minds the invention of the mechanical laws.[62]

In this view of science we see appearing many of the principles which Peirce, James, and particularly Dewey made an integral part of instrumentalism. For instance, there was the emphasis on atoms and mechanical forces as abstractions which are useful in the control of nature; there was the suggestion that man is to be treated as an integral part of the scientific environment, rather than as a spectator; and there was the denial of complete determinism, so that room could be left in cosmological theory for human free will – for the possibility of performing actions which involve an element of choice, which may have merit or deserve blame, but which are certainly not wholly determined and therefore morally neutral.

Another approach to science which loosened somewhat the tight deterministic ideal that had been the legacy of Newtonian dynamics and which also re-inforced the growing instrumentalist mode of thought, was that of William Jevons (circa 1870). Jevons made a distinction between perfect and imperfect induction. He believed that perfect induction occurred when all cases which were subsumed under the class dealt with were examined, and imperfect induction occurred when it was not possible to examine all such cases.[63] He further claimed that much of our scientific knowledge is uncertain and will remain uncertain because it is based on imperfect induction which, in its turn, depends on two principles that can never be proved: (*a*) that our past observations give full knowledge of what exists and (*b*) that nature is and will continue to be uniform.[64] Therefore, he concluded, our inferences about the future will be highly probable but never certain, and the most sensible view of scientific laws is to consider them as probability statements.[65] This last claim plus his suggestion that—

> In all cases of inductive inference we must invent hypotheses, until we fall upon some hypothesis which yields deductive results in accordance with experience.[66]

fitted comfortably within the instrumentalist mould, particularly when compared with Peirce's views on abduction (retroduction) and the role of scientific laws.[67] In this, and many other ways, the views of Jevons set the stage for the even more radical approach of Boltzmann.

Ludwig Boltzmann (circa 1900), a physicist, was concerned to explain the second law of thermodynamics on the basis of the atomic theory of matter. While attempting to show why heat cannot flow from lower to higher temperatures in a self acting manner, he came to the conclusion that the second law could be explained by combining the laws of classical mechanics with the theory of probability,[68] and in the process laid the foundations of statistical mechanics. His belief that many scientific laws were essentially statistical in nature later became fundamental to many instrumentalist creeds, as did his suggestions that philosophy and science should be firmly grounded in experience,[69] and that scientific models (theories, mind pictures) should produce consequences that are in agreement with experimental facts.[70] Boltzmann also believed that the components of these scientific models need not have existential import, and would often be nothing more than convenient mental constructs as, for example, were Newton's concepts of absolute space and time.

Another scientist who supported the mental construct view of the role of scientific theories was Heinrich Hertz (circa 1890). He saw no reason why, in principle, all the theoretical terms of science must be considered to have 'real' existence,[71] and presented a typically instrumentalist approach when he suggested that the most important role of science was to attempt the prediction of future events rather than search for the 'real' underlying structure of the universe.[72] Hertz's mental models (theories) were constrained in a variety of ways, but he asserted that we have no means of knowing whether our conceptions (mental models) of things are in conformity with things in any respect, other than that the (logically) necessary consequences of the mental models correspond to the actual consequences of the things we are concerned with. Hence, he concluded that since it is possible to have more than one theory (model) to explain the same set of facts, it may be the case that some or all of the elements of the theory will be merely mental constructs.[73] This being the case, Hertz believed that it was necessary to have some means of deciding between competing theories, and he suggested that we accept only those theories (images, models) which (a) are logically permissible, that is, are consistent with our laws of thought; (b) are correct, that is, whose essential relations are consistent with the immediate data of experience; and (c) are appropriate, that is, use the least number of empty relations.[74]

The first constraint (logically permissible) would immediately be agreed upon by most philosophers and scientists of any era, but the other two did not achieve universal assent. However, his approach did allow the possibility that theoretical entities (such as atoms that are perfectly hard, perfectly elastic, move in absolute space, etc.) need not actually exist, and thereby offered an answer to the arguments of those realists who demanded that scientific theories be not accepted unless there was reasonable certainty that they described the actual processes occurring in nature. As well, Hertz's approach did not deny the possibility that scientific theories might, in fact, describe such processes, but did suggest that we would probably not know whether they did or not. In this way, a holder of Hertz's views could avoid the realist criticism that since some entities postulated by scientific theories obviously existed (e.g. bacteria), it was highly probable that most other theoretical entities also existed.

Hertz's position also avoided the criticism that instrumentalism implies the division of scientific entities into two classes, (a) theoretical terms and (b) the rest; a division that is impossible to make in practice.[75] Such a distinction may be inferred from the Hertzian position, but is not entailed by it, and may be denied without inconsistency. As a result, this traditional criticism of instrumentalism lost much of its force.[76]

It was at this stage (circa 1890), that instrumentalism was once again becoming popular as a philosophy of science and, perhaps for the first time, there was being built up a comprehensive philosophical foundation for such an approach to science. Besides instrumentalism, it became possible to distinguish within the zeitgeist two other major philosophical movements, utilitarianism and pragmatism, which reinforced instrumentalist beliefs and which combined with instrumentalism to form one of the 'fashionable' world pictures of the day, at least in America and Europe.

Conventionalism and Instrumentalism

The conventionalist philosophies of Mach and Poincaré were another strong influence on the development of instrumentalism. Both of these men were read extensively in America, and there was a direct link to Dewey through James, who corresponded regularly with a variety of European philosophers.

Ernst Mach (circa 1890) accepted Comte's suggestion that natural philosophy had passed through the theological and metaphysical stages of thought and had become a 'positive' science based on precise observation, hypothesis, and experiment. Many of the consequences of Mach's positivist approach were incompatible with an instrumentalist philosophy, but there was one aspect of his thought which proved to be a forerunner of Dewey and the evolutionists. Mach looked upon man as a biological organism interacting with the environment,[77] and suggested that natural laws are the consequences of man's need to order and understand nature.[78] That is, they are essential because they provide economy of thought, but may be looked upon as mere subjective rules for the guidance of man's expectations.

> Absolute precision, an altogether accurate specification of the consequences of an hypothesis, can only be found in physical theory; it cannot be expected in applied physics (any more than in applied geometry). . . . Are then natural laws being nothing but subjective rules for the guidance of an observer's expectations without any value?[79]

The answer to Mach's question was 'Certainly not!' because he believed that although actuality meets with our expectations only to a limited extent, it has often proved our laws to be 'correct', even if not completely precise.

Mach's writings also emphasised two other assertions that were later to become important to instrumentalism:

a that the spectator theory of knowledge should be rejected because knowledge is derived from man's *interaction* with his environment, not from a 'detached' observation of it, and

b that it is possible to consider many scientific theories as convenient mental constructs whose logical consequences correspond closely with actual events in nature.

It is not surprising, then, to see other instrumentalist principles appearing as part of Mach's general philosophy. For instance, he suggested that a belief in the inherent simplicity and order of nature is merely a projection by man into science of the original psychological motive for scientific research.[80] It is man who is seeking simplicity and order, not nature. Or, to put it more plainly, an assertion of the type,

'Nature always works in the simplest possible manner', is an expression of *man's* desire to explain the mechanisms of nature in the simplest possible manner.

Mach further suggested that scientific laws are propositions adopted because of their ease of practical utilisation, and that science may be considered as an accumulation of instruments to test some domain of facts or precisely predict the future.[81] As well, he made virtually the same assertion as Bernard, that scientific propositions are never more than conditional, and he appeared to agree with Peirce's suggestion that a true belief is one that would tend to result from an endless scientific investigation.[82]

Another leading conventionalist was Henri Poincaré (circa 1905), but he differed from Mach in two ways. First, by suggesting that science pre-supposed an order in nature independent of man, and secondly, by attempting to prove that conventionalism did not necessarily lead to the view that science is merely the artificial creation of the scientist.[83] Both of these positions are compatible with and have proved useful to instrumentalism, but his major contribution to the growing instrumentalist tradition was the realisation that, since we cannot observe all the facts related to experimental phenomena,[84] we are forced to *select* from what is available those facts which are *worthy* of being known.[85]

This concept is important for the Instrumentalist, because it re-inforces the notion that scientific theories cannot be regarded as final.[86] Since theories are based, not on all relevant facts, but on a sample of such facts, an allowance for error and improvement is built into each theory.

Poincaré's contemporary, Duhem, also accepted this point of view, and made such a selection the first operation in his analysis of the construction of scientific theories.[87] Dewey was another who made use of a similar concept, particularly in his discussion of the process of inquiry, both scientific and otherwise.

The chemist, Wilhelm Ostwald, (circa 1905), was another scientist who argued against the 'mechanistic hypothesis',[88] but he emphasised a different aspect of what was to become instrumentalism. He was one of the first of the modern philosophers of science to assert what Dewey later made a keystone of his philosophy—that no real distinction can be made between philosophy and science,[89] because they are simply two methods leading to the some goal, the domination of nature by man. Ostwald also rejected the dualism between energy and matter accepted in the science of his day, asserting that a primary matter manifesting itself under the form of energy was the basic building block of the universe.[90] During most of his life, he also believed that the essential essence of things cannot be known by man.[91] Ostwald's work had considerable influence on the early instrumentalists. He was quoted by

James as a typical example of the application of the pragmatic theory of truth:

> Everywhere, these teachers [e.g. Ostwald, Mach, etc.] say, 'truth' in our ideas and beliefs means the same thing that it means in science . . . that ideas become true just in so far as they help us to get into satisfactory relations with other parts of our experience.[92]

and he foreshadowed both Dewey's dislike of dualisms, and his lack of belief in man's ability to know 'Antecedent Being'.[93]

Pierre Duhem, at about the same time as Ostwald, was also arguing that physical theories do not teach anything about the nature of reality. Now, Duhem, Ostwald, et al. put their case so persuasively and forcefully, that during the past seventy years this sceptical view of the nature of the relationship between theory and reality became so strongly associated with instrumentalism that it was often treated as an inescapable consequence of that philosophical attitude. However, this notion is mistaken. As was suggested in Chapter 2 and earlier in the present chapter, while an Instrumentalist may hold such a view, there is no logical necessity for him to do so.[94] For instance, Reichenbach, when discussing the question 'Are there atoms?', suggested that the same physical reality may admit of two possible interpretations—

1 That the elementary entities are assumed to be particles whose behaviour is controlled not by causal laws, but by probability laws of a form resembling waves as far as their mathematical structure is concerned. That is, the particles are materially 'real' but the waves are only mathematical quantities.
   or
2 That the waves may be regarded as physically 'real', a conception for which no particles exist.

He therefore concluded that (a) each interpretation is as 'true' as the other, (b) neither may be rejected because Heisenberg's indeterminacy principle makes a crucial experiment impossible, and, (c) both cannot be combined into one picture.[95]

Reasons of this type have often been used by Instrumentalists to justify their belief that scientific theories may, but need not, teach something about the nature of reality. However, examples such as that given by Reichenbach usually tend to lead them to suggest, as he did, that science alone may not be able to answer such fundamental questions as 'What is matter?'[96]

Certainly, Duhem took an extreme sceptical position, and viewed physical theories as no more than a system of mathematical propositions devised to represent as simply and exactly as possible a whole domain of experimental laws. He believed that 'successful' physical theories were built up by means of four successive operations, viz:

a A *selection* is made from the physical properties the scientist is concerned with, of those that are simple. These are then represented by symbols.
b Hypotheses are created to connect these symbols. These hypotheses need not express real relations and are never true or false but only approximate.
c An attempt is made to combine the various hypotheses mentioned in **b** by mathematical and logical means.
d Consequences are deduced from the hypotheses (singly or in combination) and translated back into statements about physical properties.[97]

There are two points to note here. In the first place, a noted scientist was putting forward an idea which many Instrumentalists eventually came to regard as a basic piece of dogma, namely that scientific theories are never based on all the available, relevant data.

Secondly, the organisation of the series of steps Duhem suggested for the development of physical theory bears a close resemblance to Dewey's pattern for inquiry (1920) and Campbell's analysis of physical theory (1920). In detail they are very different, but the essential overall picture—of movement from *some selected* facets of the total situation (data), to hypotheses, to conclusions which are to be tested by comparison with the behaviour of physical objects—is the same.

Another point worth noting in Duhem was his suggestion that it is inappropriate to use the words true or false with reference to scientific laws. Firstly, because, 'like the experiments on which they rest, they are only approximate,'[98] and secondly, because such laws connect symbols rather than realities and there are always cases where a symbol no longer corresponds with reality.[99]

There is little doubt that Duhem's writings contributed to the growing instrumentalist tradition, and later Instrumentalists often used his mode of reasoning to justify their beliefs. For example, Dewey supported his claim that if there is an underlying reality we may never know it, by asserting that scientific theories cannot be expected to present a picture of the 'true' reality, because,

a it is not likely that they are based on the whole of the relevant data and,
b they rely heavily on abstractions from reality.[100]

The debt to Duhem is obvious.

The Status of Scientific Theories

About the turn of the century, many writers of a variety of philosophical persuasions had come to agree with Duhem that it was inappropriate to use the terms true or false with reference to scientific theories. For example, the Realist Emile Meyerson (circa 1910), although holding a view of science which directly conflicted with that of the conventionalists, (claiming that the chief aim of science was to seek the essential nature of things, and that the discovery of rationality in nature was more important than the practical application of scientific laws) believed like Duhem that—

> . . . hypotheses could not be transformed into realities, that in their nature they were neither true nor false, that they were unverifiable in their essence.[101]

It would seem then, that at this stage in the development of science the question of the status of scientific theories and theoretical entities was developing into a major philosophical problem for Conventionalist, Instrumentalist, and Realist alike. In fact, this problem of the step from the observable to the intrinsically unobservable which had also worried Newton in the *Principia* and had led to a variety of expositions of his third rule of philosophising[102] in book three, had not been satisfactorily resolved by the end of the nineteenth century, and most philosophers, even today, find difficulty in explaining this process of 'transduction'. Certainly, the early Instrumentalists did not provide a satisfactory explanation and, in particular, the 'hard' instrumentalist line of Dewey (and the related views of the Operationalist, Bridgman) encountered considerable difficulties in this area. It is not appropriate to expand on this topic here, but when the work of John Dewey is considered in more detail in chapters four and five, the various instrumentalist solutions to this problem of the status of theoretical entities will also be discussed. To return to Meyerson.

Besides accepting that it was inappropriate to use the terms true and false with reference to scientific theories, Meyerson also highlighted another line of thought that was important to instrumentalism – the suggestion that there is a close link between the processes of common sense and the processes of scientific reasoning.[103] Meyerson's explanation for this alleged link is certainly unacceptable to most Instrumentalists, but his conclusion, that 'The elaboration of scientific hypotheses is the continuation of the process which creates the realities of commonsense . . .'[104] could have been uttered by a Dewey or a Reichenbach.

The foregoing historical outline has demonstrated that most of those

concepts that would be labelled instrumentalist by a modern philosopher were prominent in philosophic and scientific writings at various
stages in history, but particularly in the late nineteenth and early
twentieth centuries. What was always lacking, however, was a
comprehensive, coherent philosophy embracing all or most of these
ideas. An attempt at such a synthesis, based on an analysis of scientific
practice, was developed with pragmatism, and the name instrumentalism has since become associated with the founders of
pragmatism, Peirce, James, and Dewey.

Instrumentalism and the Pragmatists

As was noted in Chapter 2, Peirce, (circa 1880), a physicist, re-
examined many of the concepts fundamental to science, and produced
a controversial theory of meaning; James, (circa 1900), a psychologist,
followed him by suggesting a re-thinking of the concept of truth; but it
was Dewey, (circa 1900—1940), the philosopher and educationalist,
who attempted to produce a comprehensive philosophical system or
school of thought.

There were close personal links between the three men. Peirce and
James were members of the small circle at Harvard where pragmatism
was first formulated, and there was a close relationship between them
for the remainder of their lives. Dewey was a student of Peirce at John
Hopkins in the early 1880's; but it was James' work which converted
Dewey from Hegelianism to Pragmatism in the period 1890—1903.[105]
Although their ideas were not always compatible (e.g. Peirce's dislike of
James' interpretation of pragmatism), there were strong and obvious
connections among their basic beliefs.

Peirce, the senior member of the trio, wrote a great deal but
published relatively little.

However, he is generally credited with formulating the pragmatic
theory of meaning[106] and with attempting to move the emphasis in logic
from general to particular propositions.[107] Both innovations were to
prove important to instrumentalism.

Firstly, his belief that the way to clarify the meaning of a concept is to
examine a conditional statement of the conceivable practical consequences of the object of that concept,[108] and his suggestion that the
justification of an idea or belief is to be found in its 'cash value', that is,
the rules of action (but not particular actions) to which it led,[109] fitted
easily within the instrumentalist notion that ideas are generated
through an interaction of man with his environment. Consequently, the
pragmatic interpretation of the problem of meaning was to become a
fundamental part of many instrumentalist systems.

This pragmatic theory of meaning has been discussed and criticised at such length elsewhere,[110] that it would be merely redundant to repeat the standard arguments here. What is important for present purposes is to note that—

a   Peirce's approach to meaning and justification was largely accepted by Dewey, and through his writings became part of instrumentalism

    and

b   as was mentioned in Chapter 2,[111] this type of approach to the problem of the development of a theory of meaning appealed to scientists, because so much of their work is concerned with examining the practical consequences of theories and ideas.

The second of Peirce's ideas which was important to instrumentalism was his change of emphasis in logic from general to particular propositions. This preference for the particular is also noticeable in Dewey. Once again it is understandable that Peirce, who was well trained in physics and chemistry, and who made his living mainly from scientific work, should suggest such a move because a scientist may never forget particulars; when his mode of reasoning changes, it is often because careful observation has unearthed unexpected facts, which require the amendment of old theories or which lead to new theories, which suggest further observations, and so on.[112] This constant close interaction between theory and observations has been a continual warning to the scientist that the particular proposition is as important to him as the general law.

> The hypothesis suggested by the present writer is that all laws are the results of evolution; . . . if a law is a result of evolution, which is a process lasting through all time, it follows that no law is absolute. . . . the chance divergences from law are perpetually acting to increase the variety of the world, and are checked by a sort of natural selection and otherwise (for the writer does not think the selective principle sufficient) so that the general result may be described as 'organised heterogeneity', or, better rationalised variety.[113]

Peirce also put forward a strong argument for the uncertainty of 'truth'. He suggested that continual inquiry within a community's (scientific or otherwise) established procedures and related body of claims and beliefs would eventually lead to truth;[114] that is, truth is what is finally agreed upon by the relevant experts.[115] However, absolute truth, or stable beliefs, or perfect knowledge, or reality (these terms were synonymous for Peirce), was to be the result of an endless scientific investigation—a truly unattainable goal.[116] Consequently, Peirce believed that all current 'truths' were open to possible falsification, and all knowledge must be held to be fallible.[117]

Among his writings on philosophy, Peirce included papers on

probability, induction, abduction, and chance. Many of the ideas
contained in these works were influential in structuring William James'
(circa 1910) approach to philosophy, and particularly his concept of
truth. Reference was made in Chapter 2[118] to the suggestion that a
theory is 'true' if it 'works'. As the very brief discussion above would
indicate, this was hardly Peirce's concept of truth, but James found it a
useful idea, particularly when attempting to clarify and justify basic
moral, religious, and scientific beliefs. He made his position clear in
'Pragmatism's Conception of Truth'[119] when he suggested that, in
science, the most satisfactory way of choosing between competing
theories or 'formulas' is to—

> Find a theory that will *work*; and that means something extremely difficult;
> for our theory must mediate between all previous truths and certain new
> experiences. It must derange common sense and previous belief as little as
> possible, and it must lead to some sensible terminus or other that can be
> verified exactly. To 'work' means both these things; and the squeeze is so
> tight that there is little loose play for any hypothesis. . . . Truth in science is
> what gives us (scientists) the maximum possible sum of satisfactions, taste
> included; but consistency both with previous truth and with novel fact is
> always the most imperious claimant.[120]

Once again it should be noted that this and similar theories of truth
have been heavily criticised[121] and have encountered a number of
philosophical difficulties, but, like the pragmatic theory of meaning,
have proved useful in science. Scientists do tend in practice to accept a
scientific theory if it fits within the framework of what is already
believed without too much re-allocation or re-arrangement of fundamental laws, and if it 'works'; that is, produces predictions of future
behaviour within the limits of accuracy of the measuring instruments
available. A theory that does not 'work' is rejected out of hand. A theory
that 'works' but does not fit the current conceptual framework may be
eventually accepted, but only after much argument and controversy.
For example, the statistical explanation of the laws of thermodynamics
encountered a great deal of opposition when it was first mooted in the
late nineteenth century, and quantum theory, suggested in the late
nineteen twenties, has only recently been generally accepted by the
bulk of the scientific community. In each case, the delay was due mainly
to the fact that the acceptance of the theory required a considerable
derangement of previous beliefs.

James corresponded frequently with European philosophers and
scientists, and one of his greatest contributions to modern instrumentalism was to make himself, and hence Dewey, familiar with the
thinking of men such as Duhem and Poincaré. By the end of the second
decade of the twentieth century, there was current in both European
and American philosophy a large collection of loosely connected ideas

that could be labelled instrumentalist.[122] However, as was pointed out previously, what was still lacking was a systematic instrumentalist approach to science. This approach was provided by Dewey.

Although Dewey is not strictly a philosopher of science, many of his philosophical and educational ideas were heavily influenced by what he had observed of scientific practice and, within the framework of his general philosophy, he produced a definite, instrumentalist conception of science and its role in human intellectual progress. Certainly Dewey did not produce much that was new in the philosophy of science and relied heavily on the ideas of his predecessors, but what he did do that was of merit was to give order and cohesion to the instrumentalist attitude to science, and also draw the attention of many philosophers to the problems of fitting scientific practices and modes of thinking into traditional philosophical patterns. Modern instrumentalist analyses of science, such as those of Reichenbach and Toulmin, appear to owe a considerable debt to his work.

Because of its historical antecedents, its popularity with scientists, and Dewey's influence, by the time he produced *Logic: The Theory of Inquiry* in 1938, instrumentalism could no longer be considered a naive fad,[123] but had achieved the status of a respectable philosophy of science which had a promising future; though, even then, more as a suggestive body of ideas than as a school of thought.

NOTES

1   Reichenbach, *op. cit.*, p. 36.
2   Bronowski, J. *The Commonsense of Science*, Heinemann, London, 1960, p. 20.
3   Lovejoy, *The Great Chain of Being, op. cit.*, p. 15. My emphasis.
4   *ibid.*, p. 5.
5   Boring, E. 'The Dual role of the Zeitgeist in Scientific Creativity' in Frank, *The Validation of Scientific Theories, op. cit.*, pp. 187–97.
6   e.g. Dewey regarded his whole philosophy as instrumentalism. See also discussion by Lovejoy in the *Thirteen Pragmatisms, op. cit.*, esp. pp. 34 ff.
7   James W., 'What Pragmatism Means' in Konvitz and Kennedy, *op. cit.*, pp. 32–3.
8   *ibid*, p. 31.
9   *ibid*.
10 *ibid*, p. 34.
11 *ibid.*, p. 35.
12 Peirce, *Essays in the Philosophy of Science, op. cit.*, p. 5.
13 *ibid.*, 'The Logic of Abduction', pp. 242–3.
14 e.g. Dewey, *The Quest for Certainty, op. cit.*, Chs 1 & 2.
15 e.g. Dewey, J. *Reconstruction in Philosophy*, Beacon Press, Boston, 1968, p. vii.

16   Arguments for this claim are advanced throughout the present chapter. See also the papers by Frank, P. and Bridgeman, P. in Frank (ed), *The Validation of Scientific Theories, op. cit.*, pp. 13−25, 75−9.

17   Farrington, B. *Greek Science*, Pelican, 1944, p. 127.

18   Sophocles, *Antigone* in *The Theban Plays*, Penguin, 1964, pp. 135−6.

19   See Guthrie, W. *History of Greek Philosophy*, Vol. 2. Cambridge University Press, 1969, pp. 316−7; and Gomperz, T. *Greek Thinkers*, Vol. I, John Murray, London, 1949, pp. 219.

20   i.e. disputations as such.

21   Celsus, *On Medicine*, Introduction 8−35, trans. Spencer, W. London 1935, in Cohen, M. and Drabkin, I. *A Source Book in Greek Science*, Harvard University Press, pp. 472−3.

22   Hippocrates, *The Art*, XI. Loeb Classical Library, Harvard University Press, 1957, Vol. 129, pp. 209−11, trans. Jones, W.

23   *ibid*. XIII, pp. 213−5.

24   Hippocrates, *Ancient Medicine*, VII. Loeb Classical Library, Vol. 128, p. 25.

25   *ibid.*

26   *ibid.*, I − IV, pp. 13−21.

27   *ibid.*, I. p. 13.

28   *ibid.*, I − II, pp. 13−15.

29   Hippocrates, *Airs, Waters and Places*, Loeb Classical Library, *op. cit.*, Vol. 128, pp. 71−137.

30   Hippocrates, *Regimen on Acute Diseases*, Loeb Classical Library, Vol. 129, pp. 63−125.

31   Plato, *Timaeus*, 91. D, E, trans. Cornford, E. *Plato's Cosmology*, Routledge and Kegan Paul, London, 1966, p. 358.

32   e.g. Aristotle, *On the Parts of Animals*, II, I in McKeon, R. *The Basic Works of Aristotle*, Random House, N.Y., 1941, pp. 658−61.

33   Aristotle, *On the Heavens*, I, 2−3, 268b14−270a12 in McKeon, *op. cit.*, pp. 399−402. *Physics*, IV, 8, 215a−215a 31, in McKeon, *op. cit.*, pp. 283−4.

34   Aristotle, *On the Heavens*, I, 2, in McKeon, *op. cit.*, pp. 399−401.

35   Kuhn, T. *The Copernican Revolution*, Vintage Books, 1959, esp. Ch. 4.

36   Agricola, *De. Re. Metallica*, trans. Hoover C & H, Dover, N. Y., 1950, esp. preface, pp. xxvii − xxx.

37   e.g. Vesalius, A. *On the Human Brain*, trans. Singer, C., O.U.P., 1952, introduction by Singer, p. xviii.

38   *Ibid.*, pp. 4−6.

39   e.g., Bacon, F. *Novum Organum.*, II (IV) in. Anderson, F. (ed) Lib. of Liberal Arts, Bobbs-Merrill, N.Y., 1960, pp. 122−4, and *The Great Instauration*, IV, in Anderson, *op. cit.*, pp. 21−2.

40   Bacon, F. *Cogitata et Visa*, trans. Farrington, B. in *The Philosophy of Francis Bacon*, Liverpool University Press, 1964, p. 93.

41   *ibid.* p. 97. c/f Dewey and his views about the relationship between philosophy and science. See below, Chapters 4, 5.

42   e.g. See Smart, J. *Between Science and Philosophy*, Random House, N.Y. 1968, pp. 138−173.

43   Nagel, *op. cit.*, p. 140.

44 Helmholtz, H. *Popular Scientific Lectures*, 2nd series, trans. Atkinson, E. 1881, Dover, N.Y., 1962, p. 244.
45 *ibid*, p. 246.
46 Bernard, C. *Introduction to the Study of Experimental Medicine*, Collier Books, N.Y., 1961, p. 181.
47 c/f discussion of 'more correct' theories, Chapter 2, pp. 23–4.
48 e.g. see Nagel, *op. cit.*, p. 129 ff.
49 Bernard, *op. cit.*, p. 182.
50 *ibid.*, pp. 184–5.
51 *ibid.*, p. 192.
52 *ibid.*, p. 193.
53 *ibid.*, pp. 194–5.
54 c/f also the views of Vaihinger, H. c. 1877. Dissertation: 'Part I: Basic Principles of *The Philosophy of "As If"*.' This dissertation was enlarged, revised and published in German in 1911. Published in English in 1924. See Vaihinger, H. *The Philosophy of 'As If'*, trans. Ogden, G. London 1924, International Library of Psychology/Philosophy/Scientific Method, esp. pp. 8–13, 70–3, 217–22.
55 Stallo, J. *The Concepts and Theories of Modern Physics*, Bridgeman, P. (ed), Harvard University Press, 1960, p. 131.
56 *ibid.*, p. 136.
57 e.g. Boltzmann, p. 51 below, made it plain that in his opinion components of scientific models *need* not have existential import but he saw no contradiction in also talking about the statistical rules that describe the behaviour of atoms e.g. Boltzmann, L. *Lectures on Gas Theory*, trans. Brush, S., University of California Press, 1964.
58 e.g. see discussions in Smart, J. *op. cit.* pp. 141–55; McLaughlin, R., *op. cit.*, Chrs. 3& 4; Feigl, H. & Maxwell, G. (ed) *Minnesota Studies in the Philosophy of Science*, III, *Scientific Explanation, Space, and Time*, University of Minnesota Press, 1962, esp. the papers by Maxwell, Feyerabend, Rozeboom, Grünbaum and Sellars.
59 Boutroux, E. *Natural Law in Science and Philosophy*, trans. Rothwell, F. 1914, David Nutt., London, pp. 77–8.
    French Edition: *Bibliothèque D'Histoire de La Philosophie de L'Idée de Loi Naturelle dans La Science et La Philosophie Contemporaines*, Librairie Philosophique, J. Vrin, Paris, 1950, p. 50.
60 *ibid.*, pp. 76–7 (p. 49).
61 *ibid.*, pp. 58–9, 68, (pp. 38, 43–4).
62 *ibid.*, p. 68 (p. 44).
63 Jevons, W. *The Principles of Science*, Dover, 1958, pp. 146–8.
64 *ibid.*, pp. 149–50, 219, 228, 235.
65 *ibid.*, Ch. 11, esp. pp. 219, 224–5.
66 *ibid.*, p. 228.
67 see Chapter 2 above.
68 Boltzmann, L. *Populare Schriften*, Leipzig, 1905, pp. 345–63. Relevant sections translated by F. Bainbridge, Faculty of Arts, Swinburne College of Technology, Melbourne, Australia.
69 *ibid.*, pp. 253–70.

70   *ibid.*, pp. 261–2. See also his letter to Nature, February 28, 1895, quoted
     in the introduction to *Lectures on Gas Theory, op. cit.*, pp. 15–17.
71   c/f Vaihinger, *op. cit.*
72   Hertz, H. *The Principles of Mechanics*, Introduction pp. 1–2, trans. Jones,
     D. & Walley, J. Dover, 1956 c/f views of Dewey, *Quest for Certainty, op. cit.*,
     Ch. II and Vaibinger, H. *op. cit.*, p. 5.
73   *ibid.*
74   *ibid.*, pp. 2–3.
75   See discussions in Smart, J. *op. cit.*, pp. 141–55, esp. pp. 152–3 and
     Chapters 2, 4, 5 of this book.
76   For a more general discussion of this point see below, Chapters 4 and 5.
77   Mach, E. 'The Significance and Purpose of Natural Laws' in Danto, A.
     and Morgenbesser, S. *Philosophy of Science*, Meridian Books, N.Y., 1960,
     pp. 268–9.
78   *ibid.*, p. 270.
79   *ibid.*, pp. 272–3.
80   *ibid.*, p. 271.
81   *ibid.*, p. 272.
82   *ibid.*, pp. 272–3.
83   Poincaré, H. *The Value of Science*, trans. Halsted, B. Dover, N.Y., 1958,
     p. 140.
84   *ibid.*, p. 142.
85   Poincaré, H. *Science and Method*, trans. Maitland, F., N.Y., 1959, pp.
     15–21.
86   Poincaré, H. *The Value of Science, op. cit.*, p. 138; *Science and Hypotheses*,
     Dover, N.Y., 1952, pp. 160–5.
87   See below, pp. 55 ff.
88   Ostwald, W. *Natural Philosophy*, Williams and Norgate, London., 1911,
     trans. Seltzer, T. pp. 140–4.
89   *ibid.*, p.1.
90   *ibid.*, pp. 128, 139, 144 ff.
91   *ibid.*, pp. 4, 46–54. However, Ostwald was converted to atomism about
     1909. See Bush, S, Preface to Boltzmann, *Lectures on Gas Theory*,
     op. cit., p. 17.
92   James, W., 'What Pragmatism Means', from *Pragmatism: A New Name for
     some Old Ways of Thinking*, Longmans Green & Co., N.Y., 1907, quoted in
     Konvitz, M. & Kennedy, G. *The American Pragmatists*, Meridian Books,
     N.Y., 1967, p. 34.
93   e.g. Dewey, *Quest for Certainty, op. cit.*, Chs 1 & 2.
94   See also Nagel, *op. cit.*, pp. 137–40.
95   Reichenbach, *op. cit.*, pp. 174–5.
96   *ibid.*, p. 176.
97   Duhem, P. *Aim and Structure of Physical Theory*, trans. Wiener, P. Princeton
     University Press, 1954, pp. 19–21, 165–79 and Alexander, P. 'The
     Philosophy of Science 1850–1910', in O'Connor, D. (ed) *A Critical
     History of Western Philosophy*, Free Press, N.Y., 1965, pp. 417–20.
98   Duhem, *op. cit.*, p. 178.
99   *ibid.*

See discussion of Dewey's theories in Chapters 4 and 5.
101 Meyerson, E. *Identity & Reality*, Dover, p. 420, trans. K. Loewenberg.
102 'The qualities of bodies which cannot be intended and remitted, and which apply to all bodies on which it is possible to set up experiments, are qualities of all bodies universally.' For a full discussion of Newton's approach see McGuire, F., 'Atoms and the "Analogy of Nature"' in *Studies in History and Philosophy of Science*, May, 1970, (Vol. I. No. I), Macmillan, London, 1970, pp. 3–58.
103 Meyerson, *op. cit.*, p. 421.
104 *ibid.*
105 For further details see Wiener, P. *Evolution and the Founders of Pragmatism*, Harper and Row, N.Y.
106 See Chapter 2, pp. 12 ff.
107 Thayer, *Meaning and Action, op. cit.*, pp. 86 ff., 106 ff.
108 *ibid.*, pp. 86–100, 120–5; Peirce, C. 'How to Make our Ideas Clear in Konvitz and Kennedy, *op. cit.*, pp. 99–118, esp. pp. 107–8.
109 See discussion in Thayer, *Meaning and Action, op. cit.*, pp. 120–5. Dewey also accepted this line of thought. See *Quest for Certainty, op. cit.*, Chapter 5, esp. pp. 128–9, 136 ff and 166–7.
110 Ayer, A. *The Origins of Pragmatism*, Freeman Cooper & Co., San Francisco, Ch. 2; Thayer, *Meaning and Action, op. cit.*, Part 2, esp. Ch. I.
111 pp. 13 ff.
112 e.g. see Bernard, *op. cit.*, pp. 180 ff.
113 Peirce, C. 'Uniformity' in *Baldwin's Dictionary of Philosophy and Psychology*, N.Y., 1902. Quoted in *Essays in the Philosophy of Science, op. cit.*, pp. 164–5.
114 Peirce, C. 'The Social Theory of Logic' in *Essays in the Philosophy of Science, op. cit.*, pp. 144–54; Thayer, *op. cit.*, pp. 121 ff.
115 Peirce, C. 'How to make our Ideas Clear' in *Collected Papers of Charles Sanders Peirce, op. cit.*, Vol. V., Par. 407, p. 268. Thayer, H. *op. cit.*, p. 126–7. c/f ideas of Campbell, N. in *Foundations of Science, op. cit.*, especially Ch 8.
116 See discussion, Chapter 2, pp. 15 ff.
117 e.g. see 'What Pragmatism Is' in *Collected Papers*, Vol. 5. par. 411–437, pp. 272 ff.
118 pp. 16 ff.
119 James, W. 'Pragmatism's Conception of Truth', in Konvitz and Kennedy, *op. cit.*, pp. 44–60.
120 *ibid.*, p. 53.
121 See discussion above, Chapter 2, pp. 17 ff.
122 For details see Lovejoy, *The Thirteen Pragmatisms, op. cit.*, pp. 1–29, esp. pp. 26 ff.
123 As it was, for example, by Russell in the early decades of this century. See Russell, B. *Our Knowledge of the External World*, Allan & Unwin, London 1914, 1929. See also above, Chapter 1.

4
John Dewey

Like other animals, man adjusts to his environment; otherwise he does not live. Man's material environment, however, unlike that of the lower animals, does not consist only of land, water, air, fauna, flora, temperature and pressure. It also consists of buildings, tools, clothing, fire, vehicles, books, schools, clocks, churches, munitions, writing materials, medicines, contraceptives, machines, prime movers, and the various objects that we call material culture.[1]

Within the context of Dewey's general philosophy are found many of the instrumentalist ideas whose historical development was outlined in Chapter 3. For example, Dewey used the notion of man inter-acting with the environment as the basis of his analysis of the process of thought, and he also emphasised the idea that successful practice was the main criterion for the acceptance or rejection of scientific theories. As was suggested in Chapter 2, this approach led him to favour an attitude to science which viewed scientific theories as the products of experience, and which tended to place more stress on methods than on subject matter.[2] As well, like many of his predecessors, Dewey tended to be anti-mechanistic in attitude, and he also accepted the idea that scientific theories are not likely to be final but are always open to modification and change.[3] As support for this latter proposition, he put forward a view similar to that of Duhem—theories are never based on the whole of the original subject matter, but are developed only after the 'data' has been carefully *chosen* from this subject matter. That is, theories are based on only that small percentage of relevant subject matter which has been selected by the scientist as important for the development of a solution to the problem which was suggested by the original, 'doubtful' situation.

Other characteristics of Dewey's approach to science included an emphasis on the use of abstractions to simplify and extend scientific thought; a view of most objects of science ('physical' objects) as being merely convenient mental constructs; and a belief that scientific laws were probability statements or statistical regularities. Perhaps his overriding passion, however, was his desire to make science compatible with ethics. As Thayer points out,[4] Dewey, like Kant, Spinoza,

Descartes, and St Thomas Aquinas, was concerned to develop in one inclusive framework a reliable interpretation of both scientific knowledge and methods on the one hand, and the factors that shape ethical judgement on the other.

> Man has beliefs which scientific inquiry vouchsafes, beliefs about the actual structures and processes of things; and he also has beliefs about the values which should regulate his conduct. The question of how these two ways of believing may most effectively and fruitfully interact with one another is the most general and significant of all the problems which life presents to us. Some reasoned discipline, one obviously other than any science, should deal with this issue. Thus is supplied one way of conceiving of the function of philosophy.[5]

Consequently, Dewey's ideas about science permeate the whole of his philosophy. Also, as E. C. Moore points out,[6] Dewey's philosophical system was so built that most of its basic concepts were interdependent. As a result, it is necessary to examine many of these basic concepts before a meaningful discussion of his philosophy of science may be attempted.

As was noted in Chapter 1, Popper's assessment of instrumentalism as the thesis that scientific theories are nothing but computation rules or inference rules is hardly valid and, in the case of Dewey, is quite misleading. Dewey saw instrumentalism as a philosophical attitude which helped explain the development of science as part of the evolution of man and the refinement of his modes of thought. In his view, intelligent attempts by man to manipulate and control nature have led to what we now call science. As a result, Dewey's instrumentalism included not only his thoughts about the role of scientific theories, but also his ideas about the basic nature of reality. Let us now turn to a discussion of some of his basic beliefs.

Inquiry, Philosophy, and the Methods of Science

Dewey saw Science as the model form of knowledge, hence as an excellent example of the process of inquiry, and therefore as a paradigm which would be useful to employ in other fields of knowledge.[7] It was not surprising, therefore, that he used this scientific 'habit of thought' as the basis for his teaching method.[8]

Dewey's reasons for the esteem in which he held science were various. When discussing the process of thinking in *Essays in Experimental Logic*, he said that—

> Modern scientific procedure . . . seems to define the ideal or limit of this process [of thinking]. It is inquiry emancipated, universalised, whose sole aim and criterion is discovery, and hence it marks the terminus of our description [of the process of thinking].[9]

In *Logic: The Theory of Inquiry*, he went a step further and suggested that demands for a reform of logic are in reality a demand for a unified theory of inquiry which is based on the pattern of inquiry used in science, and which may be used generally to regulate the methods by which mankind reaches conclusions, and forms and tests beliefs.[10] Again, in *Reconstruction in Philosophy*, he asserted that scientific men have devised a method of inquiry so penetrating and useful over such a wide field of knowledge that this method of science is worthy of providing a model for inquiries in philosophy and studies in human affairs.[11] Finally, as was mentioned above,[12] Dewey saw the function of philosophy as being the development of a fruitful interaction between beliefs derived from science and beliefs about values. Consequently, his ideas about science and scientific method are not only scattered throughout his philosophical writings, but have also been deliberately woven in with his beliefs about thinking, knowing, and ethics. We shall now examine the first two of these areas—the third is largely outside the scope of this book.

Ideas and Thinking

Dewey saw all reflective thinking as a process of inquiry which involved the transformation of a doubtful situation into a settled one.

> We may carry our account further by noting that *reflective* thinking, in distinction from other operations to which we apply the name of thought, involves, 1. a state of doubt, hesitation, perplexity, mental difficulty, in which thinking originates and 2. an act of searching, hunting, inquiring to find material that will resolve the doubt, settle and dispose of the perplexity.[13]

> Judgement, understanding, conception are all of them constituents of the reflective process in which a perplexing, confused, unsettled situation is transformed into one that is coherent, clear and decided or settled.[14]

In short, Dewey was convinced that thinking of a reflective kind only occurred when the individual was confronted with a problem, 'that being in a hole, in difficulty, is the fundamental "predicament" of intelligence.'[15] Consequently, he believed that methods of solving problems, i.e. 'Inquiry', were the basis of most of mankind's intellectual achievements, and it was within this context that he looked on science as the model form of knowledge, because he considered the methods developed by science to solve its problems were the best intellectual 'tools' mankind had yet devised.

The typical form of this process of inquiry has already been discussed in Chapter 2,[16] but it is worth repeating here the basic stages envisaged by Dewey. In *How We Think*,[17] Chapters 5 to 7, he made perhaps his clearest statement of his formal analysis of the process of reflective thinking. During this discussion he made it clear that he believed that his analysis was no more than a formal analysis of an actual process in nature, and that the function of any such formal analysis or logic was not to say how we think or how we should think, but to 'set forms into which the result of actual thinking is thrown in order to help test its worth'.[18] That is, he distinguished between a psychological process designated by the name 'thinking', and an intellectual device designated by the name 'logic'. The latter was used to test or explain or support or defend the results of the process of thinking, but was not to be confused with it.[19]

Dewey analysed all processes of thinking, including scientific thinking, into five logical stages:

1 The doubtful situation which suggests the problem.
2 The analysis of the doubtful situation to define the problem and determine what information is relevant to the problem, that is, the selection of data.
3 The formulation of hypotheses (ideas) which are blue prints of operations to be performed in an attempt to solve the problem.
4 The testing and revision of the hypotheses: this may be an involved process and include extensive alterations to the hypotheses and, perhaps, even a re-definition of the original problem.
5 The solution of the problem, and the removal of the original doubt.

Dewey was careful to note that, while the above formalisation was useful for the purposes of discussion, in any real situation the number of stages might be more or less than five, and need not follow one another in a set order. He also noted that there might sometimes be a seemingly disproportionate emphasis on a single stage. As a result, he believed that no set rules could be laid down for the psychological process.[20]

Dewey's formal analysis of the process of thought stressed 'the regulative function of hypotheses (or ideas) in reason and made it easy to look upon them as intellectual tools and guides to practice. His approach led directly to the view that the universal statements constituting the laws and theories of science, function as leading principles of knowledge or rules of inference.[21] That is, they are intellectual tools for the exploration of experience—tools which might be used in a variety of ways depending upon the context, and which allow prediction, interpretation, and modification of things experienced by acting as rules in accordance with which inferences are drawn (rather than as premises from which conclusions are derived).[22]

This departure from the traditional approach to the role played by scientific theories and laws has become important to modern instrumentalism.[23] By treating theories as leading principles which are asked to do no more than allow man to reason accurately from one concrete situation to another, rather than as premises which are expected to correspond in some way with 'reality' and to lead to knowledge of the 'essence' of matter, the Instrumentalist avoids most of the problems inherent in the opposing 'Realist' position. For example, the Realist has difficulty 'interpreting' terms such as gas, electron, meson, and so forth, but for the Instrumentalist such difficulties do not exist. From his point of view, it does not matter if there are conflicting interpretations of such terms in science—if, for instance, gases are treated as continuous mediums for the purposes of acoustic phenomena, but have their thermal properties 'explained' by treating them as though they were composed of discrete particles. Nor does it matter whether the electron is treated as a particle or a wave. What matters is that, whatever 'picture' is used, the scientist keeps getting 'correct' answers. That is, answers which accord with observed phenomena, which are accurate predictions, and which allow man to control nature.

The instrumentalist view of the role played by scientific laws and theories also avoids the 'conventionalist' problem of treating the whole of science as a convenient but artificial way of explaining sense data. Treating theories as leading principles is in no way incompatible with asserting that some or all of the entities that form part of those theories are real in the sense in which the term is used by philosophers such as Smart.[24] As Nagel points out, questions can be raised about a theory when it is regarded as a leading principle that are substantially the same as those which arise when the theory is used as a premise.[25] That is, the difference between asking whether a theory is true (as a premise) or satisfactory (as a leading principle of inference) is mainly a linguistic one and therefore, since a theory may be considered to serve in either of these two capacities, the terms incorporated within the theory may be considered 'real', i.e. having existential import, by an instrumentalist as well as by a Realist.[26] As an illustration of this line of argument consider the natural law', 'metals expand when heated'. If one wishes to use this 'law' to predict the behaviour of a piece of tin when heated, one may use the traditional syllogistic method and formally argue that—

> All metals expand when heated.
> Tin is a metal.
> $\Longrightarrow$ This piece of tin will expand when heated.

However, one may equally well treat the 'law' as a leading principle, and follow the approach taken by Mill[27] and Toulmin.[28] That is, the argument would move from the given (This piece of tin is heated) to the conclusion (This piece of tin will therefore expand) in accordance with the leading principle (inference licence, warrant) that 'for any x, if x is a metal, x will expand when heated'. Consequently, unless one is influenced by an a priori preference for a particular epistemology, it would appear that the logical method used will depend largely on convenience, and therefore that the different roles assigned to laws and theories in the process of scientific inquiry by various philosophers and scientists has little or no bearing on the problem of the existential status of 'theoretical terms'—the answer to that problem would seem to lie elsewhere.

A further result of this change in emphasis on the role of laws and theories (from considering them as premises, to viewing them as leading principles) is that it allows the Instrumentalist to concentrate on the movement of scientific arguments from particular (this piece of tin is heated) to particular (this piece of tin will therefore expand) and encourages him to seek theories that allow him to predict accurately some future event from a given set of circumstances, rather than look for theories which in some way mirror or correspond with reality. However, this emphasis on the instrumental function of scientific theories does not preclude the logical possibility that such theories may mirror or correspond to reality. In fact, if the thesis expressed above is correct, and it is largely a matter of convenience which method of argument is used, the difference between the Instrumentalist and the Realist is merely a difference in emphasis, rather than a fundamental difference in kind.[29] For instance, in the case of particle physics, quantum theory allows the scientist to predict accurately the future behaviour of a sub-atomic particle such as an electron (granted that he already has knowledge of some current state for that particle) and so, for many scientists, it does not matter whether we have a physical interpretation or 'picture' of the ψ function or not, because what is most important is our ability to predict future behaviour from present behaviour, and hence modify and manipulate nature. However, this attitude is not shared by all scientists, and there are others who are industriously seeking such a 'picture'.[30]

The eventual result of these conflicts between the realist and instrumentalist positions seems to be that those philosophers who hold an instrumentalist attitude to science are likely to encourage scientists to concentrate on the development of abstract theories which have wide application and allow accurate prediction over as wide an area as possible, and may pay little or no attention to whether or not the scientist develops physical interpretations of those theories; whereas philosophers who have a realist attitude to science would be inclined to worry about possible physical interpretations of the theories of science as well as their range of applicability and accuracy of prediction. For instance, Smart exemplifies the latter attitude when he says that—

But how would we compare, let us say, a theory which was broadly correct in its ontology but whose predictions were rather inaccurate as against a theory which was incorrect in its ontology but which made fairly accurate predictions? It seems to me that there is here an unsolved problem for those philosophers who wish, as I do, to give a realistic account of scientific theories.[31]

and Dewey the former when he suggests, firstly, that—

The invention of technical symbols marked the possibility of an advance of thinking from the commonsense level to the scientific.[32]

and secondly, that—

The invention or discovery of symbols is doubtless by far the greatest event in the history of man. Without them, no intellectual advance is possible; with them, there is no limit set to intellectual development except inherent stupidity.[33]

Dewey agreed with the psychologists of his day that simplification and abstraction are necessary preconditions for coping with affairs that are complex, and he also held that the use of symbols which designate 'possible' operations has enabled man to achieve a great degree of exactness and intellectual organisation.[34] But more than this, he actively encouraged the use of abstractions because he believed that they are one of man's best aids in his search for knowledge of the basic relations upon which the occurrence of things as experienced depend, and hence assist him to gain increased control over them. That is, abstractions are essential because by their use man increases his power to regulate his relations to things as experienced, and hence to manipulate and regulate nature.[35]

At this juncture, it is instructive to look at some of the more common criticisms of instrumentalism. At various times Instrumentalists have been accused of not being keen to look for explanations beyond a low-order observational level;[36] of insisting on a rigid distinction between observational and theoretical terms, and/or between theoretical and non-theoretical terms[37] (depending on how the distinction is drawn); of looking on theoretical terms as meaningless,[38] and therefore being reluctant to introduce new terms into science;[39] and of being committed to a static science based on a fixed set of observational statements.[40]

It is beyond the scope of this book to attempt to examine these criticisms in detail, but it is appropriate to point out that they lose much of their force when applied to instrumentalist systems such as those espoused by Peirce and Dewey. Dewey's advocacy of the wide use of abstractions and mathematics in science, and Peirce's concept of the role of symbols, make nonsense of criticisms about the Instrumentalist's alleged insistence on low order explanations, and reluctance to introduce new terms into science. Also, few of the Instrumentalists whose ideas were previously discussed in Chapters 2 and 3 have insisted on a rigid distinction between observational and theoretical terms. As we shall see later, Dewey did suggest that, because of the methods of physics, the objects of physics (physical objects) cannot be individual, existential objects,[41] but he nowhere drew a rigid observational/theoretical distinction which was to be applied to all or even most scientific terms. In fact, such a distinction was quite unimportant in his system.[42] As a perusal of his explanation of the process of inquiry immediately indicates, what mattered was the conversion of a doubtful situation into a settled situation, the solution of a problem, and the only restriction placed on the method used (and hence on the theories and terms used) was that it be successful, 'solve' the problem, and remove the initial doubt.

Further, rather than regarding theoretical terms as meaningless, Dewey saw them as events. That is, as changes brought about in a system of relationships, and as effective agents for the control of nature.[43] Consequently, they were necessary if man was to reason effectively, and they had meaning because of their relationships with other terms and because of their role in inquiry.[44] But once again, the conception of a class of entities known as 'theoretical terms' is hardly useful because Dewey saw *most* nouns and numbers as symbols, as substitutes for things or relations.[45] He believed that these substitutes were detached by the intellect from the immediate situation, and manipulated to make predictions or inferences. Consequently, in Dewey's philosophy such symbols were vitally useful, because they were essential for the process of reflective thought.

> For the World of Science, especially of mathematical science, is the world of considerations, which have approved themselves to be effectively regulative of the operations of inference. It is easier to wash with ordinary water than with H_2O, and there is a marked difference between falling off a building and $\frac{1}{2}gt^2$ but H_2O and $\frac{1}{2}gt^2$ are as potent for the distinctive act of inference . . . as ordinary water and falling are impotent.[46]

It is hardly likely then, that an Instrumentalist of Dewey's persuasion would object to introducing new terms into science or be firmly committed to a static body of scientific theory. As well, as was pointed out in Chapters 2 and 3, Instrumentalists usually view scientific theories as being based on less than complete knowledge, on a 'selection' of relevant data, and therefore as being tentative and in need of constant re-examination and perhaps revision. Consequently, they are committed to a view of science which accepts change as normal—the scientist is a 'worker', a participant, caught up in an ongoing process.

Some of the detail lacking from the arguments presented above will be added later in this chapter, when an examination is made of Dewey's concept of the process of inquiry, and particularly when discussing his notions of the 'doubtful situation' and the 'data' to be used as the basis for the hypotheses which are set up to attempt to quell the original doubt.[47]

However, there is one further function of ideas (or hypotheses) in Dewey's system that should be considered at this stage. Dewey claimed that ideas are plans for possible action,[48] and he asserted that an idea is valid (rather than 'true'), if it can be used to predict future events and regulate the interactions which result in the control of the actual experiences of observed objects.[49] This line of thought led Dewey to suggest that *all* general conceptions such as ideas and theories are hypothetical, subject to change, and are to be tested by the consequences of the operations they define and direct.[50] Therefore, there was little point in his looking for a distinction between theoretical and observation terms; what he was concerned with was an examination of the function of a term/theory in inquiry, and with discovering whether or not it assisted in the resolution of the original doubtful situation which gave rise to the process of inquiry. However, if the term/theory not only helped in the solution of the original problem, but also appeared to offer a 'model' of operations actually occurring in nature, that was a bonus for an Instrumentalist like Peirce who also claimed to be a Realist, but was something of a handicap for an Instrumentalist like Dewey, who did not want to see the 'physical' objects of science competing with the objects of ordinary experience, which were ontologically prior to them. However, to a certain extent, Dewey's problem was unreal. As was pointed out above,[51] in his philosophical system, as soon as one began to talk about the objects of ordinary experience, one had to use signs which were different from, related to, but hardly rivals of, the things of ordinary experience.

The Doubtful Situation

There are two other concepts used by Dewey, the 'doubtful situation' and the original 'data', which require discussion before one can examine the role played by Thinking, Thought, and Knowledge in his philosophical system.

Within all fields of knowledge, Dewey argued against dualisms, in the sense that there could be, in principle or in fact, an irreducible separation between the methods of knowing or experiencing things and the 'natures' or 'reality' of the things themselves.[52] As Phillips has noted,[53] Dewey considered such distinctions to be *working* distinctions which were not to be taken as ontological divisions. That is, they did not exist in nature, but were created by man solely for the purpose of facilitating inquiry; and great problems arose if this was forgotten.

Some of the dualisms Dewey attacked were the traditional emphasis on the alleged separate functions of reason and sense, idea and object, theory and practice, knowing and doing, and on a division of subject matter between mind and body, ideal and real, value and fact, society and individual, environment and organism, nature and man. In each case, he was arguing for a change in attitude; from the consideration of man as a spectator, separate from nature, to the view that man was a participator, an integral part of nature.[54] This dislike of dualisms extended even to the distinction made by psychologists between stimulus and response. Madden[55] points out that Dewey conceived the stimulus to be that part of the process of inquiry which characterised a problematic (doubtful) situation that the response was designed to resolve successfully. In other words, the stimulus and response were so related that the one did not exist without the other. For this and a variety of other reasons,[56] Dewey refused to treat the individual as anything but a part of a situation, and when he spoke of a doubtful situation he was referring to the total interaction between the organism and its environment.

> If what is designated by such terms as doubt, belief, idea, conception, is to have any objective meaning, to say nothing of public verifiability, it must be located and described as behaviour in which organism and environment act together or interact.[57]

> Thinking originates in situations where the course of thinking is an actual part of the course of events and is designed to influence the result . . . since the situation in which thinking occurs is a doubtful one, thinking is a process of inquiry, of looking into things, of investigating.[58]

> . . . the actual occurrence of a disturbed, incomplete and needy *situation* indicates that *my* present need is precisely to investigate, to explore, to hunt, to pull apart things now tied together, to project, to plan, to invent, and then to test the outcome by seeing how it works as a method of dealing with hard facts.[59]

Dewey defined his basic concept, the 'situation', as follows:

> What is designated by the word 'situation' is *not* a single object or event or a set of objects and events. For we never experience or form judgements about objects and events in isolation but only in connection with a contextual whole. The latter is what is called a situation.[60]

> In actual experience there is never any such isolated singular object or event; *an* object or event is always a special part, phase or aspect; of an environing, experienced world – a situation . . . there is always a *field* in which observation of *this* or *that* object or event occurs.[61]

Now, since Dewey asserted so strongly that a situation is a special part or aspect of the total interaction of the organism with its environment, and that the organism itself is an integral part of a situation, as Phillips points out,[62] he lay himself open to the charge of subjectivism; to the criticism that the doubt or problem was unique to the mind of the inquiring organism. To refute this criticism, Dewey argued that since in practice the doubt may be removed by operations which modify existing conditions but not by merely mental processes, the doubt could not be merely a subjective state of the mind of the inquiring organism, but was a property of the situation itself.[63]

It was in this 'situation' that Dewey's dislike of dualisms led him into unnecessary complexities and obscurities. Rather than attempting to stretch the English language and prove that situations, per se, may be doubtful, he would have been better served to have pointed out that since the organism is an integral part of the situation, one may call a situation doubtful if some factor(s) in the total situation evoke doubts in the mind of the organism concerned (and would evoke doubts in the mind of any *similar* organism). Assuming that the original organism was normal for its class, one is not then committed to subjectivism because this doubt will only be removed by operations which actually modify the original, existing conditions, and there is no longer the problem of using common words in an uncommon way.

Whether or not this argument is accepted, Dewey still encounters difficulties, because, by making the organism an integral part of the situation, he then makes each situation unique, both for the participating organism and for all other organisms. That is, neither the participating organism not any other organism could exactly re-create or copy that situation. Now, to insist that each given event occurs in a unique setting may be useful to Dewey in some educational and philosophical contexts, but such a claim created some more general problems, because Dewey also desired to achieve 'objective meaning' for and 'public verifiability' of his terms.[64] In fact, to seek objectivity, but at the same time insist that the inquiring organism be an integral part of the doubtful situation and both modify and be modified by the resulting process of inquiry[65] (that is, produce a situation that cannot be exactly copied), would seem to be self-defeating.

However, over and above these difficulties, to, in principle, never be able to duplicate situations is a severe handicap for a philosopher of science, because science insists on the public verifiability of results, processes, and theories; and evidence for the acceptability of a given result is supplied by other scientists repeating the same experiments to produce the same results. In other words, in scientific practice, the inquiring organism is *not* an important part of the situation, and, even if it is an *integral* part thereof, its influence is deliberately reduced to the barest minimum by scientific procedures, which have been specifically designed to eliminate any unique influence of the human factor, the scientist. While there is no doubt that Dewey agreed with this reduction of the influence of the human factor in science,[66] and noted that this was one of the reasons why science was different from social and moral studies,[67] he did not seem to realise that there was a basic conflict between his concept of a situation and the aims of an objective science. It is probable that in his criticism of the 'spectator' theory of knowledge[68] Dewey went further than necessary; and though he may well have pointed to a flaw in contemporary philosophy by emphasising the active role of the organism in the process of inquiry, it would seem that he in turn erred by also insisting that the organism be an integral and important part of the definition of the doubtful situation itself, because this latter claim immediately created a conflict with his often stated opinion that objectivity, abstraction, and the removal of the initial matter of experience from its original setting were essential aids to intellectual progress.[69]

However, there are elements in Dewey's discussion of scientific procedure which indicate an escape from his dilemma. He suggested that not all factors in the original doubtful situation were of equal relevance or importance, and that the inquiring organism selected those factors or 'data' that seemed to him most appropriate to help solve the problem engendered by the doubtful situation.

> From the experimental point of view, the art of knowing demands skill in selecting appropriate sense data on the one side and connecting principles, or conceptual theories, on the other.[70]

Consequently, had Dewey confined his emphasis on the involvement of the organism to doubtful situations (discovery or problem states-of-affairs rather than routine states-of-affairs), where the inquiring organism obviously has an important, active role, he may well have avoided the criticisms noted above. However, he did not do this, and by insisting on the importance of the inquiring organism in all situations, including routine or testing situations where standard scientific procedures are designed to eliminate any unique influence of the inquirer, he brought his ideas into conflict with established scientific practice.

Another possible interpretation of Dewey's ideas that has sometimes been put forward is the suggestion that a situation (in Dewey's sense) would not arise until some element in the environment attracted the attention of the organism, and therefore routine or testing 'situations' would not be situations at all. However, this interpretation of Dewey's view would appear to be at variance with the quotations cited on page 75 above, and also with most current assessments of his work. Admittedly Dewey pointed out in *How We Think*[71] and elsewhere[72] that thinking only occurs when something in the environment disturbs the organism; but generally his writings do not appear to suggest that a situation, as such, only arises if some element in the environment attracts the attention of the organism.

Data

The second important term used by Dewey in a slightly unusual sense is *data*. As was noted above,[73] Dewey asserted that from the experimental point of view, knowing demanded two skills:

a   the ability to select appropriate sense data

and

b   the ability to connect the principles and/or conceptual theories that assist inquiry to reach a conclusion in any particular case.[74]

The important word in **a** is *selected*. The data do not represent all the factors which comprise the original situation, but only those selected by the organism as being relevant to (or useful for) the solution of the problem engendered by the original situation.[75] In other words, Dewey was asserting that the process of inquiry deliberately introduced a distinction between data and interpretative ideas as a means of producing an adequately tested conclusion, one we may have faith in.[76] Consequently, the distinction between data and ideas need not be fixed and, in fact, was not, because the factors selected as data and the interpretative ideas (or regulative principles) constantly checked one another and worked together to construct a new object which was then understood or known.[77] As an example, Dewey cited the case of the physician and his patient.[78] Of all the possible observations he could make, the doctor selects only those few which experience has indicated will provide most of the necessary information most efficiently. These are the *data*, and supply the evidence which must then be interpreted in the light of appropriate ideas (theories, concepts) selected from contemporary medical theory. Dewey concluded by pointing out that—

> Sense data are signs which direct this selection of ideas; the ideas when suggested arouse new observations; the two together determine his (the doctor's) final judgement or diagnosis and his procedure.[79]

Hence, although at the end of each inquiry a judgement is reached and a problem is solved, Dewey believed there was no real limit to the process, because 'In no case are the data the whole of the original object; they are material selected for the purpose of serving as evidence and signs'[80] and 'In no case do general ideas, principles, laws, conceptions, determine the conclusion'[81] because they should be used as hypotheses only.[82] Therefore, 'final' knowledge is never achieved, the process is never complete,[83] and, although the conclusion is undoubtedly warranted, it may later require revision because of changes in data, or hypotheses, or both.

Dewey further suggested that these data are generally called 'sense-data' but that this name was used only because of the role of the sense organs in their generation.[84] Once the data were selected, they might then be used as the subject matter of primitive, existential propositions, which would be unique to the inquiry which engendered them.[85] He also qualified his claim by asserting that such primitive propositions are 'primitive' in a logical but not empirical sense, and that they must be considered hypothetical because their status in inquiry was, at that stage, only tentative.

To fully understand this point it is necessary to realise that Dewey believed that the empirical primitives were the original *res* of experience—objects such as stars, rocks, trees, rain, warm and cold days, etc.[86]—which simply exist and which do not achieve the status of data until they become things which set problems, which supply question marks instead of answers, or which have become significant for some problem.

In *Essays in Experimental Logic*[87] Dewey attempted to clarify his position by drawing an analogy between *res*, data, and the objects of knowledge, on the one hand; and the undisturbed, iron-bearing rock in place in the ground, the iron extracted from this mineral rock, and the article eventually manufactured from the iron produced from the ore, on the other. That is, he compared the raw material in its undisturbed place in nature to the original *res* of experience, the metal undergoing extraction from the raw ore for the sake of being manufactured into a useful thing to the data, and the manufactured article to the final objective—the object of knowledge.

Dewey and Reality

One consequence of this process which was often stressed by Dewey was that the *reduction* of experienced things (*res*) to data involved the deliberate elimination from the *res* of their qualities and value traits. Dewey believed that the seventeenth century revolution in science which marked the change from the ancient style of a qualitative science to the modern style of a quantitative science, had produced objects of science which are not 'real' in the sense that the objects of experience are.[88] His conclusion was that such abstractions were useful, in fact, essential for the development of science, but that one must be very careful about reversing the process and making inferences about the nature of reality (which includes qualities and value traits, i.e., the reaction of the organism to the object) from the objects of science (which lack these attributes, i.e. the reaction of the organism to the object is not considered).[89]

> There is something both ridiculous and disconcerting in the way in which men have let themselves be imposed upon, so as to infer that scientific ways of thinking of objects give the inner reality of things, and that they put a mark of spuriousness upon all other ways of thinking of them, and of perceiving and enjoying them. It is ludicrous because these scientific conceptions, like other instruments, are hand made by man in pursuit of realisation of a certain interest — that of the maximum convertibility of every object of thought into any and every other . . . these ways of thinking are no more rivals of or substitutes for objects as directly perceived and enjoyed than the power loom, which is a more effective instrument for weaving cloth than was the old hand loom, is a substitute and rival for cloth.[90]

This atypical view of reality has led to some confusion, and may be one of the reasons why Dewey's views often appear to be misunderstood. However, much of the blame for such misunderstandings lies with Dewey himself, because as Thayer remarks, Dewey's refusal to use the traditional terms of philosophy in their normal way, because of the problems that he felt were built into their definitions, frequently led him into obscurities and unnecessary complexities, and often made his mode of expressing ideas unduly laboured and difficult.[91]

To summarise, in Dewey's philosophy *data* were not mere objects (stars, rocks, trees, etc.), but were things to be thought about, evidence, signs, or clues.[92] They were objects that were specially selected and stripped of their qualities,[93] so that they might serve as the starting point for reflection and inquiry.[94] Therefore, data had two main functions:

a to define and locate the problem,
and
b to furnish the clues and evidence which enabled men to solve the problem.

Relevance to Scientific Procedure

Dewey easily accommodated the scientist and his work within this general hypothesis. His suggestion was that all scientific work starts from the material of gross experience, and that once an inquiry is initiated, scientists perform two kinds of operations; firstly, a process of careful, analytic observation to select data, and secondly, a search through previous knowledge to obtain ideas to use in order to interpret the observations and suggest new experiments. These experiments then produce more observations and data, which suggest new ideas and experiments, until the problem is solved.[95] He also asserted that to facilitate inquiry, the scientist normally tried to maintain a careful but *artificial* distinction between the data and the interpretative ideas or theories which directed the experiments, whose results tested the application of those ideas or theories.[96] However, Dewey pointed out very clearly that—

> The investigator never makes the division between perceptual and conceptual material at large or wholesale.[97]

That is, he believed that the investigator does not and should not attempt to make a rigid distinction between observation statements and theoretical statements, but is careful at each stage of the inquiry to discriminate between what is, at that stage, a matter of observation and what is a matter of theory or ideas.[98] Finally, Dewey believed that when the original material was re-organised into a coherent form capable of entering into the general system of science, the process was complete.[99]

This continual interaction between theory and practice, which has been stressed throughout the above discussion, was claimed by Dewey to be the main reason for the success of science in recent centuries. Interestingly enough, it would also appear to be one of the reasons why Dewey's form of instrumentalism escapes the criticism levelled at most operationalistic/instrumentalistic theories of science by Hempel,[100] i.e. that such theories fail to attempt an explication of the logical relationships between theoretical and observational terms. As has been often mentioned in the foregoing discussions, Dewey refused to make a rigid distinction between theoretical and observational terms, and claimed that any such distinction was purely artificial.[101] Nevertheless, within his theory of inquiry, he did go to considerable lengths to explain the logical relationships between theoretical and observational terms. Whether or not his explanation was satisfactory may be a matter of argument, but he did show that it is possible to define such logical relationships, and to use these relationships to produce an explanation, not only of scientific thinking, but also of reflective thinking in general. However, before examining Dewey's explication of such relationships and the role they play in his philosophy of science, it is necessary to look at his theory of knowledge, because, as was intimated at the beginning of the chapter, Dewey's theories of inquiry, knowledge, and science are so interwoven, that an investigation of any one of these areas requires an investigation of all three.

Knowledge

To further illustrate those aspects of Dewey's theory of inquiry that have already been discussed, and to facilitate the discussion of his theory of science which follows in Chapter 5, it is appropriate now to turn to Dewey's often-expressed assertion that a need for security compels man to fasten on to the regular to control the precarious.[102] As an example of this preference for 'certain' knowledge, Dewey cited the case of the Greek philosophers during the third and fourth centuries B.C. He suggested that because the impressions made on the senses by man's continuous interaction with his environment appear at first sight to be so chaotic and difficult to control, it was no wonder that Plato and Aristotle, in search of the Greek ideal of universal knowledge, should retreat from practical experience and turn to reason as the arbiter of truth. As the Greeks saw it, the practical life was in a condition of perpetual flux[103] and it 'seemed almost axiomatic that for true knowledge (one) must have recourse to concepts coming from a reason above experience',[104] if one was to achieve knowledge, which they equated with 'eternal truth'.[105] In other words, Dewey was suggesting that if the Greeks were to control their environment and to regulate life, they were almost forced to appeal to reason in preference to experience.

> The Greeks were induced to philosophise by the increasing failure of their traditional customs and beliefs to regulate life. Thus they were led to criticise custom adversely and to look for some other source of authority in life and belief. Since they desired a rational standard for the latter, and had identified with experience the customs which had proved unsatisfactory supports, they were led to a flat opposition of reason and experience.[106]

However, Dewey believed that for much the same reason, i.e. to control and regulate life, modern man has found that the development of science and knowledge has generally relied upon the opposite concept, that the wheel has turned full circle, and we now turn to experience, both to obtain fruitful ideas about nature and to test them.

> The logical outcome is a new philosophy of experience and knowledge . . . Experience . . . is a deliberate control of what is done with reference to making what happens to us and what we do to things as fertile as possible of suggestions . . . and a means for trying out the validity of the suggestions.[107]

It was this belief that man is largely motivated by a search for security which led directly to Dewey's assertion that knowledge, per se, is a means of control, a means of making sure.[108] As a result, he developed the point of view that standardisations, formulae, generalisations, principles, universals, and so on are important parts of knowledge, because they are instruments which are used to produce better approximations to what is unique and unrepeatable.[109] Or, more generally, that objects of knowledge have been made highly abstract and not tied to immediate things, because they are then most useful as tools, instruments, and means of control.[110]

Now, whether or not a search for security is *the* motivation for man's intellectual evolution, one must allow Dewey's claim that knowledge is often regarded by man as a means of control of nature and that, to paraphrase Bacon, 'Knowledge is power'. If this notion is accepted and it is granted that—

a man desires to control nature,

and

b in the process of solving the problems that this desire entails, man has devised a very effective method of inquiry which has been developed to the highest degree in science,

then Dewey's theory of Knowledge achieves some cohesion, and becomes a far more reasonable interpretation of man's intellectual activity over the past twenty five centuries than it would otherwise seem. One may not want to unconditionally accept his claim that—

> Only that which has been organised into our disposition so as to enable us to adapt the environment to our needs and to adapt our aims and desires to the situation in which we live is really knowledge.[111]

but it is probable that there is some element of truth in what he says.

Nonetheless, Dewey's views led him into some controversial areas. For instance, he asserted that physical laws—

> Are instrumentalities in determining, through operations they prescribe and direct, the ordered sequences into which gross qualitative events are resolved,[112]

that the category of causation—

> . . . is logical, that is a functional means of regulating existential inquiry,[113]

and that, as we have already seen, logical theory—

> . . . in its usual sense is an account of the processes and tools which have actually been found effective in inquiry, comprising in the term inquiry both deliberate discovery and deliberate invention.[114]

In short, although Dewey's philosophy was an amalgamation and extension of ideas that had been current in the philosophy of science since the 1850s,[115] as the three examples quoted above illustrate, when considered as a whole it gave rise to a variety of conclusions which were at variance with the ideas of his contemporaries (but which are quite compatible with most modern views about the role of scientific laws, causality, and logic).

In particular, Dewey's organicism led to a controversial view of the nature of Knowledge, and to the assertion that—

> . . . an object as a knowledge-object is never a whole; that it is surrounded with and enclosed by things which are quite other than objects of knowledge so that knowledge cannot be understood in isolation or when taken as mere beholding or grasping of objects.[116]

As well, he looked upon knowledge as dealing with instrumental objects,[117] and took the content of knowledge to be—

. . . what *has* happened, what is taken as finished and hence settled and sure.[118]

Dewey also claimed that an object of knowledge was a 'constructed' object. That is, from his point of view, knowledge was not the grasping, apprehending, or discovering of a set of inherently fixed laws, but involved changes to what previously existed.

> Nature is intelligible and understandable. There are operations by means of which it *becomes* an object of knowledge, and is turned to human purposes, just as rivers provide conditions which *may* be utilised to promote human activities and to satisfy human need. Moreover, just as commerce, carried on by natural bodies of water, signifies interactions within nature, by which changes are affected in natural conditions – the building of docks and harbours, erection of warehouses and factories, construction of steamships and also in invention of new modes of interaction – so with knowing and knowledge. The organs, instrumentalities and operations of knowing are inside nature, not outside. Hence they are changes of what previously existed: the object of knowledge is a constructed, existentially produced, object.[119]

This attitude involved considerable difficulty for Dewey, but was consistent with his basic principles. As was pointed out earlier in this chapter, during discussions of the process of *thinking* and the concept of a *situation*, Dewey held that 'knowing' was an interaction of an organism with its environment, and did not take place in either alone, but in a situation of which they were both part. That is, within this 'situation' occurred a *trans-action* to which they both contributed.[120]

> What is known is seen to be a product in which the act of observation plays a necessary role. Knowing is seen to be a participant in what is finally known.[121]

This postulate, that knowing makes a difference to the object known, was related to Dewey's distinction between experience and knowledge, because the object as experienced was different from the object as known. Experience, he suggested, was basically what Peirce called the foreign element which forced itself 'will-he, nill-he' on man's recognition and shaped his thoughts to something quite different from what they would have been, had they followed their natural bent.[122] The things of experience were the *res* noted earlier in this chapter and had no significance as such , i.e., were not signs of anything, until some process of inquiry was introduced.[123] The things of knowledge, however, had significance, were the results of a process of inquiry,[124] and had been changed by the process of thinking. Thought was a mode of directed, overt action.[125]

Part of the confusion which this position engendered was merely terminological, and was due to Dewey's unusual use of traditional terms.[126] To look at the matter from another point of view, what, in fact, had changed during the process of knowing was the amount of information that the organism had about the object or *res*. For example, of the experienced object the organism 'knows' only its colour and shape, but of the known object the organism 'knows' a great deal more; perhaps uses to which it may be put, relations into which it may enter, and so on. That is, the result of the interaction between object and organism which Dewey called the process of knowing was *not* that the object (in the traditional meaning of the term) had changed, but that the organism's 'knowledge' of it and its relations and possible uses had grown and increased.

The consequences of this latter position (and of Dewey's position, because of his principle of interaction and his insistence that the organism is an integral and indispensable part of the doubtful situation which inquiry *changes* to a settled situation) would be that the object is changed *for this observer (organism)*, but that it (the object) retains its basic (or original) characteristics for other, similar organisms. If such were not the case, one could not explain the general consensus of opinion which is a fact of life (e.g. I, my wife, my children, and at least two friends agree, without hesitation, that this thing I am writing on is a piece of white paper crossed regularly by equally spaced horizontal blue lines), and which Dewey and many other Instrumentalists require as a test of 'truth'.

Enough has been said above to suggest that it is probable that Dewey would basically agree with this re-statement of his position but, as Thayer has argued,[127] Dewey was so intent on avoiding dualisms that, rather than make a strong distinction between organism and environment, he went to the other extreme and ran the risk of being seriously misunderstood by appearing to ignore the individual altogether. Whatever the truth of the matter, for a variety of reasons which included his dislike of dualisms and also a desire to avoid the criticism that he was really referring only to subjective states of mind, Dewey asserted that emotions like fear (or doubt, or joy, and so on) were properties of reality, of the world.[128] However, he still retained his problem, because his use of the term 'reality' included the concept 'reality as perceived by the organism involved in the situation'.[129] For instance, if an experienced soldier, a raw recruit, and a rat stood side by side and experienced almost the 'same' set of circumstances during a battle, it could well be that the soldier would accept the 'situation' as normal, largely lacking in fearsome qualities, and would carry out a certain appropriate set of duties; the recruit would see the 'situation' as fear-inspiring, and be close to panic; while the rat might accept the 'situation' with joy and anticipation of a bountiful supply of food in the near future. Consequently, the point would seem to be that fear is not a property of reality as such, but is dependent upon the organism experiencing that reality. Now, it might well be that Dewey could have countered such criticisms by asserting that, in the three cases cited above, although the three organisms stood in almost the same place and experienced virtually the same conditions, the three 'situations' were different (according to his definition of 'situation'). However, it would seem less misleading to accept some distinction between organism and environment, and talk of 'a particular set of circumstances evoking a fear feeling (reaction?) in this organism', rather than to say that 'the situation is fearful'—that is, to look on fear as product of the environment rather than as a function of the environment.[130]

Despite the difficulties noted above, Dewey adhered to his unusual definitions of reality, situation, and knowledge throughout his long philosophical life. One reason for this persistence in the face of considerable criticism would seem to have been his acceptance of a biological archetype as the basis of his overall conceptual model. This aspect of his organicism now requires some explanation.

The Biological Model

Moore points out[131] that Dewey's attitude to philosophy developed at least partly as a consequence of his opposition to the 'spectator' theory of knowledge,[132] and Phillips notes[133] that Dewey's acceptance of an organismic model considerably influenced his thinking. Thayer further suggests[134] that Dewey's ideas about the characteristics of living things in general influenced his ideas about man and man's 'quest for certainty', and was an important factor in structuring his theory of knowledge.

Let us look then at the starting point for Dewey's theory of knowledge, his claim that 'living things constantly feel needs and make an effort to satisfy them.'[135] This deceptively simple claim becomes far more complex when the terms are properly defined. *Needs* were equated with a condition such that the organism was in an uneasy or unstable equilibrium of energies; *effort* meant movements which acted on the environment in ways which reacted on the organism to restore its characteristic pattern of active equilibrium; and *satisfaction* was the recovery of *an* equilibrium pattern after changing the environment.[136]

These typically biological/psychological concepts do seem to have had a marked effect on the structure of Dewey's philosophical writings. The analogy between his definition of *effort* and his acceptance of *knowledge* as a means of control is immediate and obvious. In fact, the quotation used previously to illustrate Dewey's views about the nature of Knowledge—

Only that which has been organised into our disposition so as to enable us to adapt the environment to our needs and to adapt our aims and desires to the situation in which we live is really knowledge.[137]

is really only an elaboration of his basic claim that 'living things constantly feel needs and make an effort to satisfy them.'

These quotations make manifest Dewey's feeling about the whole of nature (animate and inanimate) and how it works. Throughout his writings he accepted as his model for the interactions between man and nature the interactions of a simple biological organism with its environment. And as Passmore notes,[138] when comparing Dewey with James, it is this interaction of man with nature which is the keystone of Dewey's philosophy. From such a model the basic concepts of instrumentalism may easily be derived—for example, the model immediately suggests that it is appropriate to view knowledge as a means of control, that ideas and general principles are tools or instruments to further this control, and so on.

The model is also related to Dewey's pattern of inquiry. The definition of *needs*, given above, bears a close resemblance to the starting point for inquiry, the 'doubtful' situation. And it is not difficult to equate 'an uneasy or unstable equilibrium of energies' with a state of 'perplexity, confusion, doubt due to the fact that one is implicated in an incomplete situation whose full character is not yet determined'.[139] When Dewey was explaining the connection between the intellectual and practical studies, he suggested that—

> . . . the combination of what things *do* to us . . . in modifying our actions, furthering some of them and resisting and checking others, and what we can do to *them* in producing new changes constitutes experience. The methods of science by which the revolution in our knowledge of the world dating from the seventeenth century, was brought about, teach the same lesson. For these methods are nothing but experimentation carried out under conditions of deliberate control.[140]

That is, the organism, man, reacts to changes in his environment in an attempt to recover an equilibrium and to produce a settled situation.

Schematically the comparison may be made as follows:

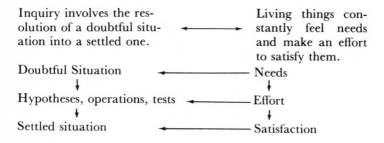

This biological model explains most of Dewey's fundamental beliefs—why Dewey claimed that knowing is a kind of action;[141] that all branches of knowledge are fundamentally similar in origin, nature, and intent;[142] that science is the paradigm for all knowledge,[143] because it is the most successful form of knowledge, and so on. Thus experimental knowledge became for him a mode of doing,[144] a mechanism of occurrences,[145] and, in scientific procedure, he believed that knowing *was* doing.[146] Dewey put his point of view succinctly, when he said—

> In other words, it is only needed to conduct such an operation as the pouring of an acid on a metal for the purpose of getting knowledge instead of for the purpose of getting a trade result, in order to lay hold of the principle upon which the science of nature was henceforth to depend . . . the first thing was to alter and extend the data of sense perception: to act upon the given objects of sense by the lens of the telescope and miscroscope, and by all sorts of experimental devices. To accomplish this in a way which would arouse new ideas (hypotheses, theories) required even more general ideas (like those of mathematics) than were at the command of ancient science. But these general conceptions were no longer taken to give knowledge in themselves. They were implements for instituting, conducting, interpreting experimental inquiries and formulating their results.[147]

Knowing and Doing

It might be argued that in this type of system the body of knowledge would be in such a state of flux that man's 'quest for certainty' could not be achieved. However, Dewey, with some justification, did not accept this as a valid criticism. He saw clearly that there must be a body of conserved knowledge to give the starting point for inquiry and to act as a reservoir of ideas and hypotheses; in short, to provide the base on which man might build new knowledge. However, he changed its role. Like Bernard,[148] he did not treat conserved knowledge as an end in itself, but asked it to fulfil the role it plays in modern science, to act 'only as a means to learning, to discovery'.[149] In fact, a characteristic of Dewey's writing was his continual attack on the traditional view which he alleged saw knowledge as something to be memorised, and thinking as divorced from action. He regularly reverted to his basic theme that—

> Genuine intellectual integrity is found in experimental knowing. Until this lesson is fully learned, it is not safe to dissociate knowledge from experiment nor experiment from experience.[150]

> That all knowledge, as issuing from reflection, is experimental (in the literal physical sense of experimental) is then a constituent proposition of this doctrine. Upon this view, thinking, or knowledge getting, is far from being the armchair thing it is often supposed to be.[151]

Consequently, from Dewey's point of view there was no easy road to knowledge. Knowledge was equated with work; knowledge meant thinking; the objects of (scientific) knowledge were the solutions to problems set by data,[152] i.e., were the conclusions of reflective inquiry,[153] in short, knowledge was active not passive. Hence the name 'objects of knowledge' was reserved for—

> Subject matter so far as it has been produced and ordered in settled form by means of inquiry; proleptically objects are the *objectives* of inquiry.[154]

This conclusion led Dewey to make the characteristically instrumentalist claim that, in principle, all knowledge is fallible[155] because the objects of knowledge are the results of (scientific) inquiry[156] (i.e. are the consequences of experimentation,[157] the *deliberate* rearrangement of nature), and therefore what is known is still only an hypothesis which must be re-adjusted, if necessary, when new discoveries are made.[158]

As a corollary to this claim, Dewey put forward the related suggestion that, because there is no fixed eternal knowledge, the *method* of obtaining knowledge was more important than the knowledge itself.[159] This change in emphasis, from the knowledge itself to the methods used to obtain that knowledge, is another characteristic of Dewey's point of view, and would seem to serve some 'useful' purpose in discussions about science, provided it is remembered that, like knowledge, the methods used are themselves likely to stand in constant need of revision, and should be replaced or re-adjusted when necessary.

Dewey claimed for his point of view two advantages:

a that it removed the traditional gulf between theory and practice,[160]

and

b that it led to workable definitions of 'good' and 'value'.

That is, Dewey considered that an object of knowledge was *good* if it satisfied the conditions which induced the inquiry,[161] and that the *value* of an object of knowledge depended upon the quality of intelligence (that is, the method[162]) used to reach it. Man was to judge knowledge by what was done to get it, not by what was said.[163]

> If we judge the work of a scientific inquirer by what he does and not by his speech when he talks about his work (when he is likely to talk in terms of traditional notions that have become habitual) we shall have little difficulty, I think, in accepting the idea that he determines the cognitive claims of anything presented to him on the basis of the method by which it is reached.[164]

Now, these are problem areas which are beyond the scope of this book, and they are merely mentioned here to indicate the overall consistency of Dewey's point of view and to demonstrate how his ubiquitous biological model spread into most aspects of his philosophical system.

NOTES

1   Allen, F. et al, *Technology and Social Change*, Appleton, Century, Crofts, N.Y., 1957, p. 7.
2   c/f. Boutroux, *op. cit.*, and Ostwald, *op. cit.*
3   c/f. Bernard, *op. cit.* and Peirce, *op. cit.*
4   Thayer, *Meaning and Action, op. cit.*, pp. ix, 165. It is interesting to note that Dewey's concern for the relationship between knowledge and ethical judgements is reflected in much of the current literature concerned with the interaction of technology and society. For example, see Mesthane, E. *Technological Change*, Mentor, N.Y., 1970, esp. Chapter 2.
5   Dewey, *Quest for Certainty, op. cit.*, pp. 18–19. See also pp. 255–6.
6   Moore, E. *American Pragmatism*, Columbia University Press, N.Y., 1966, pp. 190 ff.
7   e.g. *Quest for Certainty, op. cit.*, pp. 50, 198.
8   Dewey, *How We Think, op. cit.*, p. v.
9   *Essays in Experimental Logic, op. cit.*, p. 216. My additions in brackets.
10 *Logic: The Theory of Inquiry, op. cit.*, p. 79.
11 *Reconstruction in Philosophy, op. cit.*, pp. xxix, xxx.
12 p. 67–8
13 *How We Think, op. cit.*, pp. 12.
14 *Ibid*, pp. 165.
15 *Influence of Darwin on Philosophy*, Indiana University Press, Bloomington, 1965. See also *How We Think*, pp. 99 ff, and *Logic; Theory of Inquiry*, p. iii.
16 pp. 17–20.
17 *op. cit.*
18 *How We Think, op. cit.*, pp. 73. For other detailed references and argument see above pp. 19–24.
19 See above, pp. 19–24 esp. pp. 20–21.
20 See above, pp. 19–20, *How We Think, op. cit.*, p. 116.
21 c/f Toulmin's 'Warrants', Toulmin, S. *Uses of Argument*, Cambridge University Press, 1958, pp. 98 ff.
22 See discussion in Thayer, *op. cit.*, pp. 376 ff and Nagel, *op. cit.*, pp. 129 ff.
23 See discussion in Nagel, *op. cit.*, pp. 134 ff.
24 Smart, *op. cit.*, ch. 5., esp. pp. 133–7.
25 Nagel, *op. cit.*, p. 139.
26 For example see Reichenbach, *op. cit.*, Ch. 2, esp. pp. 176–90 with special reference to p. 186.
27 Mill, J. *A System of Logic*, Longmans Green, London, 1884, Ch. 3, Sect. 3–4, pp. 121–8.
28 Toulmin, *Uses of Argument, op. cit.*, esp. Ch. 3.
29 For example, compare the interpretations of reality given by the

Instrumentalist Reichenbach, *op. cit.*, Ch. 2 and the Realist, Smart, *op. cit.*, pp. 133—5.

30 Nagel's exposition of an argument similar to that given above (Nagel, E. op. cit., pp. 138—9) has been criticised by Sellars on the grounds that Nagel is being subtly instrumentalistic when he equates both 'true' (as a premise) and 'satisfactory' (as a technique of inference) with 'leading to conclusions which are in agreement with facts of observation to some stipulated degree'. (Sellars, W. 'Scientific Realism or Irenic Instrumentalism' in Cohen, R and Wartofsky, M. (ed.) *Boston Studies in the Philosophy of Science*, Vol. 2. Humanities Press, N.Y., 1965.) However, there is no doubt that, in common philosophical usage, when one speaks of a scientific concept as true, one means, among other things, that the concept in question leads to conclusions which accord with observations to some stipulated degree. Similarly, as was pointed out in Chapter 2, the Instrumentalist, when he speaks of a scientific concept as satisfactory, means, among other things, that the concept in question leads to conclusions which accord with observations to some stipulated degree. It is hardly instrumentalistic of Nagel to point out this fact. As well, this criticism has no bearing whatever on Nagel's main assertion that it is only a matter of convenience whether an argument is constructed using a scientific theory as a premise or as a rule of inference. It is true that G. E. Moore (*Philosophical Studies*, Routledge and Kegan Paul, London, 1922, Chapter 3) also attacked this type of argument by suggesting that a theory's leading to conclusions which are in agreement with facts of observation to some stipulated degree (or leading to fruitful conclusions etc.) is how we *recognise* true theories—it is not what makes them true. However, undoubtedly the instrumentalist would reply, 'You misunderstand. Of course that is how we recognise true theories. That is what makes them true *for us*.'

31 Smart, *op. cit.*, p. 135.
32 Dewey, *Quest for Certainty, op. cit.*, p. 152.
33 *ibid.*, p. 151.
34 *ibid.*, p. 217.
35 *ibid.*, pp. 218—9.
36 e.g. McLaughlin, *op. cit.*, pp. 245.
37 e.g. Sellars, W. 'Language of Theories' in Feigl, H. and Maxwell, G. *Current Issues in the Philosophy of Science*, Holt, Rinehart and Winston, N.Y. 1961, pp. 57—76; Smart, *op. cit.*, pp. 141—55; McLaughlin, *op. cit.*, pp. 30—1, 147—9.
38 Smart, *op. cit.*, pp. 141—2; Maxwell, G. 'Ontological Status of Theoretical Entities', *Minnesota Studies in the Philosophy of Science III*, 1962, pp. 3—27; McLaughlin, *op. cit.*, p. 243.
39 McLaughlin, *op. cit.*, pp. 237, 249.
40 Smart, J. *Philosophy and Scientific Realism*, Routledge and Kegan Paul, London, 1963, Ch. 2. McLaughlin, *op. cit.*, pp. 249, 259.
41 For example, *Quest for Certainty, op. cit.*, pp. 241, 248.
42 And would have been against a life long tendency to attack distinctions or dualisms. See Phillips, D. 'John Dewey and the Organismic Archetype'

in Selleck, R. (ed) *Melbourne Studies in Education, 1971*, M.U.P., 1971.

43 *Quest for Certainty, op. cit.*, pp. 218—9.

44 Dewey, *Essays in Experimental Logic, op. cit.*, p. 433.

45 *ibid.*, pp. 432 ff, *Quest for Certainty, op. cit.*, pp. 128—9.

46 *Essays in Experimental Logic, op. cit.*, pp. 434—5.

47 See below.

48 *Quest for Certainty, op. cit.*, pp. 155. See also discussion, above, pp. 21 ff.

49 *Quest for Certainty, op. cit.*, p. 129.

50 *ibid.*, pp. 165—7, 114.

51 p.73.

52 *Quest for Certainty, op. cit.*, Chs 2, 10. For a comprehensive discussion of this point see Thayer, *Meaning & Action, op. cit.*, pp. 172 ff; Moore, E. *op. cit.*, pp. 190 ff; Blake, et al, *Theories of Scientific Method*, University of Washington Press, 1966, pp. 279 ff.

53 Phillips, D. C. 'John Dewey & the Organismic Archetype' in Selleck (ed) *Melbourne Studies in Education*, 1971, *op. cit.*, esp. pp. 250—4.

54 *Quest for Certainty, op. cit.*, pp. 23—5. This somewhat radical approach may be traced directly to Chauncy Wright. See Madden, E. (ed), *The Philosophical Writings of Chauncy Wright*, American Heritage Series, Liberal Arts Press, N.Y., 1958, p. 4.

55 Madden, E. 'Chauncy Wright and the American Functionalists' in Blake, *op. cit.*, pp. 278—80.

56 See Phillips, *Organicism and its Influence on . . . Dewey, op. cit.*, Ch. 6.

57 Dewey, *Logic: The Theory of Inquiry, op. cit.*, pp. 33.

58 Dewey, *Democracy and Education, op. cit.*, p. 148.

59 Dewey, *Essays in Experimental Logic, op. cit.*, p. 70.

60 Dewey, *Logic: The Theory of Inquiry, op. cit.*, p. 66.

61 *ibid.*, p. 67.

62 Phillips, *Organicism and its Influence on . . . Dewey, op. cit.*, pp. 183—4.

63 Dewey, *Logic; Theory of Inquiry, op. cit.*, pp. 105—6.

64 See quote from *Logic: Theory of Inquiry, op. cit.*, p. 33, cited above p. 75, and *Experience & Nature, op. cit.*, p. 30.

65 For discussion of Dewey's claim that the inquiring organism both modifies and is modified by the process of inquiry see Phillips, *Organicism and its Influence on . . . Dewey, op. cit.*, pp. 173, 184 and Moore, E. pp. 193 ff.

66 e.g. see *Quest for Certainty, op. cit.*, pp. 152, 157—9, 217.

67 e.g. *ibid.*, 216—7.

68 e.g. ibid, pp. 213—5. For further discussion of Dewey's 'primary paradox' see Moore, E. *op. cit.*, pp. 193 ff.

69 e.g. *Quest for Certainty, op. cit.*, pp. 130 ff, 152, 157—9, 217. See also discussion below pp. 78 ff. concerning 'data'.

70 *Quest for Certainty, op. cit.*, p. 172.

71 op. cit., Chs 1, 5, 7.

72 e.g. *Quest for Certainty, op. cit.*, p. 189, *Logic: The Theory of Inquiry, op. cit.*, Ch. 6.

73 Quotation p. 77.

74 *Quest for Certainty, op. cit.*, pp. 172—5.

75 e.g. *ibid.*, pp. 172—5, 179, 261. *Experience & Nature, op. cit.*, pp. 25, 29. The

fact that such selection is an integral and important part of scientific inquiry has often been noted by philosophers. A recent example would be Schwab, J. in his essay 'The Structure of the Natural Sciences', Ford and Pugno, *op. cit.*, pp. 31–49, esp. pp. 37–9.

76 *Quest for Certainty, op. cit.*, pp. 173.
77 *ibid.*, pp. 172–5, 178–9.
78 *ibid.*, p. 174.
79 *ibid.*, p. 175; see also p. 178.
80 *ibid.*, p. 175.
81 *ibid.*
82 *ibid.*, c/f views of Bernard, *op. cit.*
83 c/f views of Peirce, *op. cit.*
84 *Quest for Certainty*, p. 179.
85 *ibid.*
86 *ibid.*, p. 99.
87 *op. cit.*, p. 35 ff.
88 *Quest for Certainty, op. cit.*, pp. 137, 90, 94, 177.
89 *ibid.*, pp. 136–7.
90 *ibid.*, pp. 135–6.
91 Thayer, *Meaning and Action, op.cit.*, pp. 173–4.
92 *Quest for Certainty, op. cit.*, pp. 99.
93 *ibid.*, pp. 90, 94, 137, 177, 179, 261; *Experience & Nature, op. cit.*, pp. 25, 29.
94 *Quest for Certainty, op. cit.*, pp. 99, 178.
95 *ibid.*, p. 173.
96 *ibid.*
97 *ibid.*, p. 174.
98 *ibid.*
99 *ibid.*
100 Hempel, C. 'A Logical Appraisal of Operationism' in Brody, B. (ed), *Readings in the Philosophy of Science*, Prentice Hall, N.Y., 1970, pp. 202–4.
101 Therefore the strongest criticisms by Smart and McLaughlin of instrumentalism are refuted. See above pp. 72 ff.
102 e.g. *Quest for Certainty, op. cit., passim; Experience and Nature, op. cit.*, pp. xi, 47, 57, 67.
103 Dewey, *Democracy and Education, op. cit.*, p. 263.
104 *ibid.*, p. 272.
105 *ibid.*, p. 263.
106 *ibid.*, pp. 275–6.
107 *ibid.*, p. 273. Note the similarity to his concept of scientific method – see Chapter 5.
108 *ibid.*, pp. 272, 275–6, 341; *Quest for Certainty, op. cit.*, pp. 100, 106; *Experience and Nature, op. cit.*, p. 154.
109 *Experience and Nature, op. cit.*, pp. 117, 152.
110 *ibid.*, p. 129; *Democracy and Education, op. cit.*, p. 341; *Quest for Certainty, op. cit.*, pp. 100, 106.
111 Dewey, *Democracy and Education, op. cit.*, p. 344.
112 Dewey, *Logic: The Theory of Inquiry, op. cit.*, pp. 454–5.
113 *ibid.*, p. 462.

114 Dewey, *Essays in Experimental Logic, op. cit.*, p. 20.

115 See above, Chapter 3.

116 *Essays in Experimental Logic*, p. 32. For a full discussion of the problems involved in Dewey's organicism, see Phillips, *Organicism and its influence on . . . Dewey, op. cit., passim.*

117 *Experience and Nature, op. cit.*, p. 152.

118 *Democracy and Education, op. cit.*, p. 341.

119 *Quest for Certainty, op. cit.*, pp. 210—11.

120 Dewey, J. & Bentley, A. *Knowing and the Known*, Beacon, Boston, 1949, pp. 323—4. For discussion of this concept, see Phillips, *Organicism and its influence on . . . Dewey, op. cit.*, pp. 170 ff.

121 Dewey, *Quest for Certainty, op. cit.*, p. 204.

122 Dewey, *Influence of Darwin on Philosophy, op. cit.*, pp. 202—3.

123 For a discussion of this position, see Moore, E., *op. cit.*, pp. 195—7.

124 Dewey, *Quest for Certainty, op. cit.*, pp. 183, 198, 242.

125 *ibid.*, pp. 111, 166—7.

126 See discussion above, pp. 78—81.

127 Thayer, *Meaning and Action, op. cit.*, pp. 171—4.

128 Dewey, *Experience and Nature, op. cit.*, p. 42.

129 Moore, E. *op. cit.*, pp. 209—12, notes this problem, but unfortunately offers no criticism of Dewey's position.

130 This latter is, of course, Dewey's position. See *Experience and Nature, op. cit.*, p. 42.

131 Moore, E. *op. cit.*, pp. 193—4.

132 e.g. see Dewey, *Quest for Certainty, op. cit.*, pp. 21—3.

133 Phillips, D. C. 'John Dewey and the Organismic Archetype', *op. cit.*

134 Thayer, *Meaning and Action, op. cit.*, pp. 178 ff.

135 Dewey, *Experience and Nature, op. cit.*, p. 252. The same point is made in *Logic: The Theory of Inquiry, op. cit.*, pp. 26—7.

136 Dewey, *Experience and Nature, op. cit.*, pp. 252—3.

137 Dewey, *Democracy and Education, op. cit.*, p. 344.

138 Passmore, *op. cit.*, pp. 115 ff.

139 Dewey, *Democracy and Education, op. cit.*, p. 150.

140 *Ibid.*, p. 272.

141 Dewey, *Quest for Certainty, op. cit.*, p. 167.

142 *ibid.*, pp. 220, 226—7.

143 *ibid.*, pp. 51, 72, 106, 250.

144 *ibid.*, p. 102.

145 *ibid.*, p. 24.

146 *ibid.*, pp. 24, 102, 107, 194, 214, 255, 276.

147 Dewey, *Democracy and Education, op. cit.*, pp. 272—3.

148 See above, Chapter 3.

149 Dewey, *Democracy and Education, op. cit.*, p. 149.

150 Dewey, *Essays in Experimental Logic, op. cit.*, p. 74.

151 *ibid.*, p. 13.

152 Dewey, *Quest for Certainty, op. cit.*, pp. 99, 122.

153 *ibid.*, pp. 183, 198, 242.

154 Dewey, *Logic: The Theory of Inquiry, op. cit.*, p. 119.

155   *Quest for Certainty, op. cit.*, p. 193.
156   *ibid.*, pp. 103, 181, 192, 200.
157   *ibid.*, pp. 86, 242.
158   *Experience and Nature, op. cit.*, p. 154.
159   *Quest for Certainty, op. cit.*, pp. 204, 214−5.
160   *ibid.*, p. 171.
161   *ibid.*, p. 197.
162   *ibid.*, pp. 200, 213−5, 245−6.
163   *ibid.*, pp. 200, 215, 221, 234.
164   *ibid.*, p. 200.

5
Dewey
and Science

The view of society as a tension-management rather than as a self-equilibrating system has distinct advantages in making *both* order and change problematical, but also 'normal'. Tensions – or inconsistencies and strains, if the word 'tensions' is too subjective or has too psychological a connotation – are intrinsic to social systems, not simply accidental accompaniments or the product of changes that impinge on the system from external sources. Once the tensions characteristic of all or of particular types of social systems are identified, they are predicted to be the probable sites of change. Now, as an equilibrium model would indicate, the predicted change may well reduce the strain. And the postulate that social action is interconnected – that it is to be analysed in terms of a system – permits hypotheses to be formulated concerning the effects of particular changes, the secondary consequences, including those that come full circle and make additional alterations in the original tension point.[1]

Like Duhem, Dewey claimed that science was not concerned with ultimate reality (that is, with the discovery of knowledge about a fixed, antecedent Being),[2] and that modern science had rejected the traditional idea that only the immutable could be real.[3] He also noted, long before it was fashionable to do so, that science may achieve and measure only a high degree of probability,[4] and therefore maintained that the ultimate test of scientific theories had become their correspondence with gross experience.[5] On the other hand, he realised that man's 'quest for certainty' would continue to lead him to a search for absolutes, and to a preference for 'exact' studies such as mathematics or mechanics[6] or physics rather than an 'inexact' science such as psychology.[7] Finally, he viewed mathematics as essential to science, and believed that although mathematical symbols designated symbolic operations or relations, the 'meaning' of these operations/relations still lay in concrete situations.[8]

Probably because of his concern with science as the paradigm form of inquiry, Dewey was led to define science as—

Knowledge that accrues when methods are employed which deal competently with problems that present themselves.[9]

He realised that this definition was so broad that it would admit as a science practically any organised, human behaviour,[10] but he was

willing to accept this consequence of his definition because, as has
already been noted, he viewed 'science' as the major element in modern
man's quest for certainty and successful struggle to control nature.[11]
Dewey also used this latter belief to explain science's emphasis on causes
and causal relationships. However, Dewey's notions about causality
differed somewhat from the classical view because he defined a causal
relationship as the *sequential order itself*, not the last (or first) term which
may be the initial (or last) term in another sequential order,[12] and he
suggested that the attitude that a cause is intrinsically more primary
and necessary than an effect is understandable, but wrong in essence.[13]

The argument that Dewey was criticising here used 'cause' in the
sense of an *antecedent* which, when manipulated, regulated the
occurrence of a *consequent*, e.g. in electrical theory the relationship
$E \propto R$. That is, potential difference is directly proportional to resistance,
provided that temperature, current, etc., remain constant. If R is
manipulated, E changes in a predictable fashion. Therefore, runs this
argument, a change in R is the *cause* of a change in E (the effect). Dewey
agreed that in this type of situation an emphasis on R (the cause) rather
than E (the effect) was understandable, because manipulation of R may
be used as a method of control of the behaviour of E, but he asserted that
it was neither R nor E that was important. Rather, it was the 'order' or
relationship $E \propto R$ which mattered. However, he acknowledged that
man's practical bias toward the regular and repeated, his 'Quest for
Certainty', would probably always lead to a preference for 'causes'
rather than 'consequences'.[14]

Scientific Theories and Gross Experience

As has already been mentioned,[15] Dewey asserted that the validity of
scientific theories should be tested by comparing the conclusions of such
theories with the results of ordinary observation, not by comparing
them with some form of antecedent Being; that is ' . . . all scientific ideas
go *back* to sense perceptions previously had for both their origin and
their warrant'.[16] As a result, he held that the basis of science was the *res*
of experience—stars, rocks, trees, what man can do, etc.[17]—and
therefore he considered that the objects of common sense had a double
status, viz:

a When they precede the operations of inquiry, they are not
knowledge but data.[18]
b When viewed as the consequences of the operations of inquiry,
they are objects of knowledge.[19]

That is, Dewey believed that reflective knowledge (science) began and
ended with the things of gross experience which were their *only* means of
regulation,[20] that knowledge and experience were inexorably linked

together.

> It is in this sense that all reflective knowledge as such is instrumental. The beginning and the end are things of gross everyday experience. But apart from knowledge the things of our ordinary experience are fragmentary, casual, unregulated by purpose . . . by making abstractions and generalisations we ascertain certain basic relations upon which the occurrence of things experienced depend. . . . But we return from abstractive thought to experience of them with added meaning and with increased power to regulate our relations to them.[21]

As well, he argued that the process of reflection (inquiry) altered the things of experience in the sense that they then ceased to be isolated and became parts of a system, and, like Bernard, Dewey believed that there were many observations that would not have been made if a theory had not been used as a guide to observing them. For example, he cited the special set of observations of an eclipse of the sun that were made to check Einstein's hypothesis that light would be deflected by a large mass.[22]

Basically, then, Dewey's position was that scientific theories and the things of gross experience belong to one organically complete system, and he also argued strongly for the 'reality' of the things of gross experience. More will be said later concerning his preference for the objects of experience, when his general concept of reality and the relation he postulated between 'physical' (scientific) objects and 'real' objects are discussed.

Science — Concepts and Ideas

Dewey followed the lead of Bridgman and Eddington,[23] and accepted that the meaning of a scientific concept was defined by a set of operations.[24] He was strongly critical of opposing points of view, particularly those of Newton. He claimed that Newton's discrete, sensory definitions of scientific concepts were entirely mistaken,[25] because scientific concepts are derived from the observed consequences of experimental operations, and therefore cannot be inherent properties of objects (like Newton's absolute space, time, and motion) but are relations of events.[26] Furthermore, he suggested that scientific concepts are instruments which direct the operations of experimental observations,[27] and that, like other types of concepts or ideas, they must be considered as systems of hypotheses which are worked out under conditions of definite test, and by means of which man might better control nature.[28] That is, scientific concepts are like other instruments and are hand-made by man for some particular purpose. One important result of this 'hand-tooling' of scientific concepts by man was the claim noted above, that scientific concepts have deliberately been made abstract to ensure the maximum amount of translation from one concept to another.[29]

Hypotheses

As was mentioned previously when discussing his notion of the process of thinking, Dewey considered that scientific (and other) hypotheses were instrumental to inquiry[30] and were employed as directive ideas for making new observations and experiments. That is, they were intellectual tools.[31] In this way he believed that scientific hypotheses had exactly the same status as all other types of ideas, concepts, and theories.[32] They were essential to inquiry, but were tentative, and should never be believed absolutely, but should be looked upon as plans for possible action, and were to be tested by comparing the results they predicted with the consequences of experiment.[33] However, despite his emphasis on testing and experimentation, Dewey did not fall into the trap of supposing that the verification of hypotheses was the whole purpose of the process of inquriy—he realised fully that such verification was merely one part of the process.[34] He also tended to follow the philosophical attitude of Boltzman and Duhem by suggesting that, providing the results of an hypothesis proved to be useful and were accurate predictions, there was little point in arguing about whether or not the objects of the hypothesis had actual 'existence'.[35] In fact, he claimed that the *worth* of an hypothesis was independent of the existential status imputed to its subject matter, because hypotheses advanced knowledge even if they were later rejected.[36] And to some extent the history of science supports Dewey's thesis, because mistaken ideas such as the phlogiston theory, and the concept of electrical/magnetic 'fluids', and Ptolemy's mathematically complex but useful geocentric universe have often performed useful roles in science.

Relations

Dewey appears to have accepted the Hegelian idea that an object is made what it is by its relations, and he placed considerable emphasis on the role played by relations in scientific work. Firstly, he suggested that modern philosophy has taken from the Greeks the idea of inquiry as the scheme of logical relationships among existences.[37] Secondly, he believed that since science is interested in understanding those changes which are the beginnings of inquiry,[38] it was then only a short step to man's considering the chief aim of science to be the discovery of the properties and relations of things (which could then be used as instruments and as means to ends),[39] rather than the revelation of their inner nature or 'essence'.[40]

A consequence of this attitude was Dewey's belief that in seeking to uncover the 'mechanism' of nature, science had inevitably come to concern itself with the discovery of constant relations among changes, and that it was these constant relations which constituted the proper subject matter for science.[41] That is, problems are solved, not when the scientist achieves some type of correspondence between his theories and a form of antecedent Being, but when the observed changes are interconnected,[42] the constant relations discovered,[43] and the laws proclaimed.[44] As a typical example, Dewey cited the case of the colours red and green. In commonsense discourse, these are simply two different colours, but in scientific discourse the names *red* and *green* refer to two different lines in a spectrum—and from the scientific viewpoint that is all that *red* and *green* do mean, any qualitative 'meanings' are avoided.[45]

Dewey further extended this line of thought by asserting that modern science creates a gulf between the objects of science and the objects of experience. He argued that scientists deliberately use instruments and apparatus to remove the qualitative aspects from the matter of direct perception. They then use the processes of thought to change the objects of observation to objects of knowledge,[46] firstly, by quantitatively assessing the conditions and effects of their occurrences, and secondly, by disclosing relations not otherwise apparent.[47] To emphasise his point, Dewey noted that for Aristotle, quantity was an accident and qualities fundamental, but that at least since the time of Descartes, scientists have considered quantity as the essence of matter, and qualities as being of secondary importance.[48]

Dewey believed that it was by means of this removal of qualities from the objects of perception (and thereby freeing these objects from the connotations with which habit and custom would otherwise have overlaid them) that scientific method made abstraction and generalisation possible, and hence allowed free movement from one concept to another.[49] Furthermore, he believed that it was by the use of standardised measurement techniques and mathematics that scientists *deliberately construct* scientific concepts so that they can achieve the maximum translation from one concept to another.[50] Such an organisation was possible when operations were considered as relations, because then they were independent of the overt instances in which they were exemplified. However, Dewey preserved his pragmatic outlook by also reminding the reader that the meanings of such operations were found in the possibility of such over actualisations.[51]

Basically, then, it would seem that what Dewey was highlighting was the simple fact that the scientist uses observed co-existences as the basis for the development of non-observed, inferred sequences. Consequently, in this sense at least, data and theory could be said to be inseparable, but there need not necessarily be a direct logical connection between them. As a typical example Dewey cited the procedures followed by a geologist when dating a fossil.[52] He noted that even with the most sophisticated modern techniques, including carbon dating, the age of fossils cannot (yet?) be measured directly, and that the geologist must use observed relations such as the fossil's relationship to other artefacts found in the same stratum, the relationships of the various strata to one another, and so on, to make inferences about the possible age of the specimen.

Scientific Objects

The mode of reasoning outlined above led Dewey to one of the more controversial areas in his philosophy of science, namely, his beliefs about the role of scientific objects. However, in some ways his views were relatively straight-forward. For instance, his two suggestions in *Experience and Nature*[53] are quite conventional. Firstly, he claimed that scientific objects such as atoms, after a series of increasingly complex relationships, give rise to qualities such as blue, sweet, pain, beauty, etc.; and secondly, that scientists postulate such 'physical' objects as atoms to explain causal relationships by demonstrating that such relationships form the conclusions of an ordered series or theory.[54] The reason he gave to explain the use of these 'mental constructs' or 'physical objects' in science was that this procedure has allowed scientists to successfully control the behaviour of ordinary things.[55] That is, like the objects of the Arts, 'physical' or 'scientific' objects are an order of relations which serve as tools by means of which man may regulate events.[56] As a result, 'physical' objects have usually been formulated in terms of space, time, and motion so that man might create broad, flexible schemes concerning nature and its workings.[57]

It was because Dewey saw scientific (physical) objects as being made by man to ensure the maximum translation from one concept to another[58] that he asserted that they do not have the same uses and values as the things of direct experience,[59] and it was at this stage in his pattern of reasoning that Dewey's beliefs about scientific objects began to depart from what was considered conventional for his time. As has already been mentioned, he was concerned to preserve the primary status of the objects of experience or 'real' objects, and frequently suggested that scientific (physical) objects were not rivals for real objects for a number of reasons.[60] For example—

a Concepts such as cells, electrons etc., are meaningless[61] unless related to observed or experienced objects.[62]

b Scientific objects are only a means of regulating the objects of experience.[63]

c Scientific objects do not include sensory consequences.[64]

d   Scientific objects are intermediate between uncertain and settled
     situations,[65] and have been created by man to simplify, classify and
     help inquiry.[66]

Dewey also asserted that because of the nature of scientific (experimental) method, which defined scientific objects by 'operations that are
interactions', such objects could not have fixed characters.[67] In Chapter
9 of the *Quest for Certainty*, he carried this view to its logical conclusion
when he stated that—

> The procedure of physics itself, not any metaphysical or epistemological
> theory, discloses that physical objects cannot be individual existential
> objects. In consequence, it is absurd to put them in opposition to the
> qualitatively individual objects of concrete experience.[68]

It would seem then, that Dewey believed that scientific objects
were (*a*) only correlations of changes,[69] or (*b*) sets of measure-
ments of relations between two or more qualitative objects,[70] or
(*c*) statements of the relations between sets of changes a qualitative
object sustains with changes in other things;[71] and that the reason for
the postulation of scientific objects is the assistance such concepts give to
man's quest for certainty and intellectual security by broadening the
extent of his control over nature[72] (as do all the products of reflective
thought).

Several comments may be offered about this point of view. In *The
Quest for Certainty*,[73] Dewey asserted that—

> What science actually does is to show that any natural object we please may
> be treated in terms of relations upon which its occurrence depends, or as an
> event, and that by so treating it we are enabled to get behind as it were, the
> immediate qualities the object of direct experience presents, and to regulate
> their happening, instead of having to wait for conditions beyond our control
> to bring it about. Reduction of experienced objects to the form of relations
> which are neutral as respects qualitative traits, is a pre-requisite of ability to
> regulate the course of change, so that it may terminate in the occurrence of
> an object having desired qualities.

As well, in *Essays in Experimental Logic*,[74] he was at pains to point out that
the basic brute facts or *res* of experience were useless as such because
they lacked significance, were not signs of anything, and only achieved
significance in inquiry after' . . . they have been extracted for a
purpose—for the purpose of guiding inference'.[75]

In this sense, then, it was possible for Dewey to maintain a distinction
between (*a*) 'natural' objects (in his terminology) which had no
significance and no use, (*b*) data, and (*c*) scientific and other
intellectual objects or objects of knowledge which had significance, had
some definite role in the process of inquiry, and were therefore useful.

However, it is to be noted that the difference was basically a difference in role; a difference in the object's relationship with man; a matter of whether the object was useful to him or not. One is brought once again to the realisation that what might be *res* for one man might well be *data* for another, and that the 'nature' of an object in Dewey's sense depended very much on its role in inquiry, and hence on the inquiring agent. According to Dewey's view, one is forced to accept the human element as an essential part of the total situation, and therefore must accept a certain amount of subjectivity in one's definitions and distinctions. However, as was noted above,[76] Dewey was so anxious to avoid the dualisms that would result (*a*) from treating inquiry (doubt, judgement, etc.) as mental states or personal traits, or (*b*) from regarding the human organism and the environment as separate objects, that he was willing to run the risk of being misunderstood by refusing to use terminology which clearly indicated that some human element was an essential part of his basic unit, the 'situation'.

However, Dewey's biological model and his dislike of dualisms were not his only reasons for not wishing to consider scientific laws and theories as descriptions of the universe and its parts, and hence for doubting the 'existence' of scientific objects. Dewey also objected to the idea of a completely ordered, mechanistic world, and was concerned to preserve room for freedom of action by the human agent.[77] He believed that chance was a real factor in the universe, and, as a result, he welcomed both the statement of Heisenberg's uncertainty principle and Maxwell's assertion that atomic theories were based on statistical methods.[78] Using these concepts as support, he asserted that—

> Since constant relations among changes are the subject matter of scientific thought, that subject matter is the mechanism of events. The net effect of modern inquiry makes it clear that these constancies, whether the larger ones termed laws or the lesser ones termed facts, are statistical in nature. They are the products of averaging large numbers of observed frequencies by means of a series of operations. They are not descriptions of the exact structure and behaviour of any *individual* thing, any more than the actuarial 'law' of the frequency of deaths of persons having a certain age is an account of the life of one of the persons included in the calculation.[79]

This statement does not in itself imply a lack of belief in the existence of scientific (physical) objects, but a little earlier in the same chapter Dewey used the 'statistical' argument to support his assertion that the 'physical' object could not be taken to be a single or individual thing in existence—that the procedure of physics itself disclosed that 'physical' objects could not be individual, existential objects.[80] His argument may be paraphrased as follows: This table exists and is real,[81] but 'the table' is an abstraction.[82] The scientific or physical object is an extension of the same process, is a further abstraction, and consists of standardised relations or interactions.[83] Consequently, these standardised constants should not be treated as the reality of nature.[84] For example, although considering 'the table' as a 'swarm' of molecules is a very useful concept and widely instrumental, this fact does not imply that those molecules, those 'physical' objects, are 'real'.[85]

Now, one may well agree with Dewey that many scientific laws are basically statistical in nature and that the basis of atomic physics is also statistical, without agreeing with his conclusion that 'physical' objects do not have individual existence. For instance, his own argument from the statistical nature of scientific 'laws' or 'facts' quoted on page 103 above, does not preclude the existence of individual, physical objects. However, it does suggest that it is not possible to *predict* exactly the behaviour of an individual particle or physical object. To use his own example: undoubtedly an actuarial 'law' does not offer an account of the life of one of the persons included in the calculation, but it certainly does not preclude the possibility that people exist (in fact, this particular 'law' pre-supposes that they do exist.) Similarly with scientific laws. They may not allow the scientist to fully account for or measure the behaviour of an individual particle, but they certainly do not preclude the possibility that such particles exist. In fact, it does not seem to be at all inconsistent to assert both that such particles exist and that they may also be regarded (or used) as standardised relations or interactions. Dewey admitted that there might be some form of antecedent Being,[86] but, as we have already seen, he also asserted that we can never know it.[87] Consequently, although it may have been reasonable for him to assert that the idea of existence for 'physical' objects was not a useful concept, it was not reasonable for him to extend the argument to include the assertion that 'physical' objects, *per se*, cannot exist.

Scientific Objects and Reality

A further difficulty with Dewey's argument was his use of the words 'real' and 'reality'. As was noted above,[88] Dewey suggested that whereas one may predicate qualities (colour, aroma, beauty, etc.) of 'real' objects, the scientist deliberately excludes qualities from scientific objects to obtain the maximum amount of objectivity and translatability from one concept to another. As a result, he believed that scientific objects could not be classified as 'real' objects,[89] and so, in one sense, there was no conflict between Dewey's concept of scientific objects (or objects of thought) and contemporary practice in either science or philosophy. What had happened was that, once again, his 'odd' use of traditional terms had led to linguistic difficulties and to a great deal of unnecessary confusion. Nonetheless, there is little doubt that Dewey's ideas about scientific objects from one of the least satisfactory elements in his philosophy of science.

In his own account of his point of view,[90] Dewey summarised his beliefs as follows.

The objects of science exhibit four main characteristics:

a They are spatial—temporal orders which may be expressed mathematically, and are therefore *constant* and in marked contrast to the variability of qualities, immediate events, and so on.

b They are so constructed that extensive substitutions and translations are possible. That is, with the help of mathematics and symbolic manipulation and abstraction, man so uses the objects of gross experience that the control and accurate prediction of the behaviour of natural phenomena become feasible.

c They (objects of knowledge)[91] are means or tools.[92] Therefore, fundamental units such as atoms and electrons are important because they are used to explain and regulate individual events, but they need not have any existential import.

d (Almost a re-statement of **a, b,** and **c**). Since they (scientific objects) are instrumental, laws are important because they are expressions of the relations which are the constancy among variations, and allow man to control phenomena.

Science—Inquiry and Methods

Dewey believed that the principle on which science was based was that one knows an object when one knows how it is made.[93] He also believed that in the process of discovering how objects were made, man devised a method of inquiry whereby he came to know by doing:[94]

> . . . in science the question of the advance of knowledge is the question of *what to do*, what experiments to perform, what apparatus to invent and use, what calculations to engage in, what branches of mathematics to employ or to perfect, so *the* problem of practice is what we need to *know*, how shall we obtain that knowledge and how shall we apply it.[95]

As a result, Dewey claimed that the essence of scientific inquiry was experimentation—to introduce change, and see what other change ensued. Or, if the phenomena studied made the introduction of change impossible,[96] to alter the conditions of observation.[97] That is, the scientist began inquiry by controlling experience in various ways,[98] but mainly by manipulating natural existences and reducing them to the status of means or tools.[99] Dewey also pointed out that all experimentation involved *overt* doing,[100] and that experimentation was not a random procedure, but was directed by ideas.[101] The outcome of this process of scientific inquiry he believed to be a new situation ' . . . in which objects are differently related to one another, and such that the *consequences* of directed operations form the objects that have the property of being *known*'.[102]

Dewey further claimed that the emphasis by science on an overt, highly specified mode of experimentation[103] had led to a co-operative tendency towards consensus because honest empirical inquiry specified when, where, and why selection of data and ideas took place, thereby enabling others to repeat the experiment and test its worth.[104] However, he was careful to point out that the purpose of scientific thinking was not to eliminate choice, but to use the notion of the achievement of a consensus to render such choices less arbitrary and more significant.[105] That is, Dewey felt that if most of the relevant experts agreed that 'x' was significant, then 'x' *was* significant.

Further, Dewey saw the purpose of experimentation as being considerably more than the mere verification of hypotheses.[106] Although he believed that the 'truth' or 'falsity' of ideas depended on the results of experimentation,[107] and that experiments were of value because of the fact that they confirmed, refuted, or modified an hypothesis, he felt that the most important result of experimentation was the extension and expansion of current knowledge.[108] That is, using the terminology discussed above in Chapter 4,[109] Dewey believed that experimentation (like any other process of inquiry), while turning a problematic situation into a resolved or settled one, would bring to light new objects of knowledge, and thereby add depth, range, and fullness of meaning to the objects of ordinary experience.[110]

Another reason for Dewey's approval of the methods used in science was that he believed scientists had produced outstanding results, opened up new fields of subject matter, and created new techniques of observation without reference to any external authority or to some form of antecedent Being[111] (because scientific inquiry had generated its ideas within its own procedures and tested them by its own operations).[112] Of course, from Dewey's point of view, a significant part of these procedures and one which he often stressed as an important reason for the success of science, was the translation of observed co-existences into non-observed, abstract, and inferred sequences,[113] which were then checked by reproducing in experiment what had been inferred. This was the case, for instance, with the example cited previously, concerning the procedures of geologists, who, when learning how to date fossils accurately, put wood (and other materials) under conditions of extreme heat, pressure, and so. on, to determine what structural changes will occur, in what sequence they will occur, and how long they will take to occur, to help determine the worth of their theories.[114]

A further example used by Dewey concerned Galileo's work on dynamics. Dewey noted that from his observations of naturally moving bodies, Galileo derived some hypotheses about motion in general, then set up experiments with balls rolling down smooth inclined planes to test these hypotheses, and used the results to confirm his idea that 'rest' was not the natural state for a body.[115] However, Dewey felt that what was important in Galileo's procedure was not so much his revolutionary assertion that bodies do not naturally come to rest because of their own intrinsic tendency to fulfil an inherent nature, but his extension of his ideas to cover the idealised situation of a frictionless ball on an unlimited, perfectly flat, horizontal plane. Dewey believed that this latter procedure was especially noteworthy, because it not only marked a departure from contemporary scientific thinking, but also opened the way for the description of natural phenomena in terms of space, time, mass, and motion. As a result, this new approach to science had readily lent itself to the extensive use of mathematical procedures, which had enhanced the possibility of translation from one concept to another, and had eventually led to the Newtonian system of dynamics and the realisation that 'the movements of the planets obey the same mechanical laws of mass and acceleration as mundane bodies'[116].

For Dewey this was a turning point in history, because he believed that from the time of Newton onwards man was gradually able to discard teleological explanations and thoughts of purpose in nature[117] in favour of a previously unattainable ideal—the belief that nature both could and should be controlled for man's benefit.[118] In fact, Dewey saw the increasing intellectualisation and abstraction of science that had occurred since the seventeenth century as the direct result of the success of Galileo's innovation in producing an improvement in subsequent attempts to control nature.[119] As a result, Dewey accepted this change in scientific thinking as a revolution in man's whole attitude to nature—a revolution which not only transformed science, but which spread its effects widely through all branches of knowledge.[120]

> When the things which exist around us, which we touch, see, hear and taste are regarded as interrogations for which an answer must be sought (and must be sought by means of deliberate introduction of changes till they are re-shaped into something different), nature as it already exists ceases to be something which must be accepted and submitted to, endured or enjoyed, just as it is. It is now something to be modified, to be intentionally controlled. It is material to act upon so as to transform it into new objects which better answer our needs. Nature as it exists at any particular time is a challenge, rather than a completion; it provides possible starting points and opportunities rather than final ends.[121]

In short, Nature ceased to be the arbiter of man's fate and became something which set problems, the solutions of which led to the modification and control of nature. In this way, the objects of ordinary perception were seen, not as something final, but as staring points for reflection and investigation—as starting points of inquiry.[122]

Once he had come to these conclusions, Dewey's course was obvious. Scientific method was another form of the process of inquiry, and his analysis of scientific method naturally followed very closely his analysis of the process of inquiry in general.[123] He claimed that scientific inquiry started from the problems set by man's everyday environment which provided the data, the material *deliberately selected* by the scientist concerned, because he thought it would throw light on the problem confronting him.[124] The analogy he used here was the case of the doctor examining a patient.[125] The doctor does not attempt to measure every one of the patient's natural functions, but concentrates on those few such as pulse, temperature, and respiration that experience and training have suggested to him are relevant to making an inference about the nature of the patient's ailment.[126] That is, the *observations* which make up the experienced whole are reduced to the *data* which locate the nature of the problem.[127]

Overall, Dewey suggested that the process of scientific inquiry usually demonstrated five main stages which were not necessarily mutually exclusive and which need not appear in a rigidly fixed order.[128] These stages were:

1:   The original problem.

2:   The selection of data. In the process of selecting data, qualities are eliminated because, in science, data means objects minus qualities.[129]

3: a   The data evoke the thought of operation (s) which may resolve the doubt which originated the inquiry.[130]

   b   These thoughts, (ideas or hypotheses) direct a search for the relations or interactions:

     1   Upon which the occurrence of real[131] qualities and values depend,

     2   by means of which man can regulate and control their occurrence.[132]

4:   The scientist's conclusions (hypotheses) about the relations which determine the occurrence of natural events are then tested against primary experience by means of experiment.[133] It is in this context that Dewey developed his ideas about logic, and was eventually led to claim that deduction, as a concrete operation, was the act of taking and using 'that which is selective, experimental, and checked constantly by consequences'.[134]

5: a   Finally, the original material is re-organised into a coherent form capable of entering into the general system of science.[135] The problem is solved.

b The problems unearthed in the process of this empirical method
usually lead to more investigations and more knowledge.[136] In
fact there was no real limit to the process, because the data was
never the whole of the original object, and the general ideas and
laws never fully determined the conclusion, because they were
used as hypotheses only.[137]

As would be expected from what has already been said, the process just
described is identical with the standard method of inquiry discussed
above in Chapter 4,[138] and it is unnecessary to repeat here the criticisms
and comments that were a part of that discussion. It is interesting to
note, however, that although Dewey was not strictly a scientist,[139] he
did claim that his philosophy was based upon actual scientific practice
and many of the comments of contemporary scientists about their
methods supported his claim. A typical example is Ostwald, whose
description of scientific method in *Natural Philosophy*[140] approximates
quite closely to Dewey's description of the process of thinking. Further
support for Dewey's claim comes from the fact that, as has been
emphasised throughout this book, Dewey's philosophy incorporated
many ideas which were first put forward by practising scientists in the
last half of the nineteenth century.

Dewey and Newton

An illuminating illustration of Dewey's general attitude to science is
provided by the fact that he highly praised the work of Galileo,
Descartes, and Hobbes, but, unlike most commentators on the history of
science, was somewhat critical of Newton. His preference for the former
trio rested on the belief that they had led a revolution in science because
they rejected the Aristotelean approach of their contemporaries and
refused to consider qualities as primary and therefore standing in no
need of explanation. Instead, they looked on qualities as problems and
challenges to inquiry, and then attempted to describe and explain
natural phenomena by using 'masses in motion'[141] (as did Newton at a
later date).[142] However, despite Newton's insistence that his methods
were empirical, Dewey claimed that Newton often erred by reverting to
'metaphysics' instead of persisting with the use of experimental method.
He believed that this was especially the case when Newton made the
assumption that his conceptions could be explained by postulating the
existence of ultimate, unchangeable substances which interacted
without undergoing change in themselves. Dewey found it impossible to
reconcile the idea of immutable Newtonian atoms which moved in
absolute space and time with his own conclusion that all conceptions
and intellectual descriptions must be formulated in terms of operations,

actual or imaginatively possible.[143]

Dewey had some justification for this criticism of Newton, who was never able to vindicate his belief in 'corpuscles' as the ultimate units of matter.[144] Furthermore, Dewey was able to support his criticism by appealing to Einstein's call for a concept of simultaneity which was based on experiment and not assumption; so that temporal relations would come to be measured by the consequences of an operation in the field of observed phenomena, and would become a relation of events, rather than an inherent property of objects.[145]

Dewey was much influenced by Einstein and by the impact on science of the special theory of relativity. He claimed that two of Newton's basic postulates were contradictory and in asserting both that

1   the position and velocity of any body can be determined in isolation from all others,
    and
2   all particles continuously interact,

Newton was asserting an impossibility. Dewey believed that Heinsenberg's uncertainty principle pointed out this contradiction and conclusively demonstrated that Newton was mistaken, because the continuous interaction of the sub-atomic particles prevented the accurate measurement of both the position and velocity of an electron at the same time.[146]

Scientific Laws

Dewey's conclusions about the Newtonian system were consistent with the more general instrumentalist mode of thought which had now been part of the zeitgeist for some seventy years,[147] and he continued to be true to the instrumentalist pattern when he asserted that his criticisms of Newton led to the conclusion that mass, position, and velocity are all relative. Therefore, he concluded, nothing is immutable (a non-sequitur), and consequently laws are merely formulae for the prediction of the probability of an observable occurrence. That is, laws designate relations which are thought of in such a way that man can predict those probabilities.[148]

As was noted above in several places, this idea led to the attitude that scientific laws, like other ideas, concepts, and so on, were to be regarded (*a*) as intellectual tools or instruments,[149] (*b*) as mere hypotheses,[150] and (*c*) as statistical expressions which could not offer a description of the behaviour of any individual things.[151] In other words, while scientific laws might express dialectic intent, their main purpose was to suggest methods to regulate and control the flow of unique situations.[152] As might be expected, this conception of the role of scientific laws re-inforced Dewey's belief that science should make full use of abstractions and mathematics so that this control might be facilitated.[153]

To summarise, from Dewey's point of view—

> Scientific conceptions are not a revelation of prior and independent reality. They are a system of hypotheses, worked out under conditions of definite test, by means of which our intellectual and practical traffic with nature is rendered freer, more secure and more significant.[154]

Conclusion

For a variety of reasons that are outside the scope of this book, Dewey's version of one of the most influential modes of thought current in philosophy of science in the first quarter of the present century has never been given the status it perhaps deserved, even though many of the ideas he advocated have since been espoused by philosophers and scientists such as Ostwald,[155] Campbell,[156] Sullivan,[157] Bridgman,[158] Reichenbach,[159] Nagel,[160] and Frank.[161] However, there is little doubt that Dewey's ideas about science are worthy of study from a variety of different points of view. In particular, they are of interest to the Educationalist and Sociologist, as well as to the Philosopher of Science. Firstly, because modern science appears to be replacing the simple cause-and-effect Newtonian type of world picture with a Dewey-like awareness that many causes constantly producing varied effects make up the complicated, everchanging, and dynamic systems that constitute nature (including human society);[162] secondly, because of the considerable influence Dewey's philosophy of science has had on recent American thinking in many fields through its role as the basis of his educational philosphy; and thirdly, because of the emphasis modern science curricula (particularly at the secondary school level) place on an understanding of the structure and methodology of science[163] and the exalted value such curricula often place on that which they term *the* scientific method.

Finally, it is fitting to conclude this book by quoting Dewey's own assessment of the role of the 'scientific attitude of mind' in that activity most essential for the continued existence of any society—education.

> Our teachers find their tasks made heavier in that they have come to deal with pupils individually and not merely in mass. Unless these steps in advance are to end in distraction, some clue of unity, some principle that makes for simplification, must be found. This book represents the conviction that the needed steadying and centralizing factor is found in adopting as the end of endeavour that attitude of mind, that habit of thought, which we call scientific. This scientific attitude of mind might, conceivably, be quite irrelevant to teaching children and youth. But this book also represents the conviction that such is not the case; that the native and unspoiled attitude of

childhood, marked by ardent curiosity, fertile imagination, and love of experimental inquiry, is near, very near, to the attitude of the scientific mind. If these pages assist any to appreciate this kinship and to consider seriously how its recognition in educational practice would make for individual happiness and the reduction of social waste, the book will amply have served its purpose.[164]

NOTES

1   Moore, W. *Social Change*, Foundations of Modern Sociology Series, Prentice Hall, 1969, pp. 10–11.
2   Dewey, *Quest for Certainty, op. cit.*, p. 47.
3   Dewey claimed that this latter view had only developed because of man's quest for certainty and hence for 'certain' knowledge. See *Quest for Certainty, op. cit.*, pp. 21–2.
4   *ibid.*, p. 27.
5   *ibid.*, p. 57. That is, he refused to accept the overriding importance of the other popular tests for the truth of scientific theories, e.g. agreement with some authority like Aristotle, the Bible, Newton, etc; compatibility with the current set of theories or mode of thought; a 'mirroring' of ultimate reality; and so on.
6   *ibid.*, p. 28.
7   *ibid.*, pp. 26, 206.
8   *ibid.*, pp. 150–6, 160–1.
9   *ibid.*, p. 199.
10 *ibid.*
11 *ibid.*, pp. 128–9.
12 *Experience and Nature, op. cit.*, pp. 99–100. c/f ideas and comments expressed above concerning *Situations*, pp. 74 ff.
13 *Experience and Nature, op. cit.*, p. 109.
14 *ibid.*, p. 114. For a more detailed exposition of Dewey's viewpoint see *Logic: The Theory of Inquiry*, Ch. 22
15 p. 96
16 *Quest for Certainty, op. cit.*, p. 115; see also pp. 72–3, 89 and *Experience and Nature, op. cit.*, pp. x, 2a, 14, 23.
17 *Experience and Nature, op. cit.*, pp. 2a, 4a, 8.
18 See above, p. 78
19 Dewey, *Quest for Certainty, op. cit.*, p. 198.
20 *ibid.*, pp. 218–9.
21 *ibid.*
22 *Experience and Nature, op. cit.*, p. 5.
23 See *Quest for Certainty*, p. 111, notes 1 and 2.
24 *ibid.*, pp. 111, 118–9. As is well known, this point has led to considerable academic argument, e.g. see Smart, *Between Science and Philosophy, op. cit.*, p. 138 ff. and Brody, *op. cit.*, p. 182 ff.
25 *Quest for Certainty, op. cit.*, pp. 115 ff, 145.
26 *ibid.*, p. 146.

27   *ibid.*, p. 192.
28   *ibid.*, p. 165.
29   *ibid.*, pp. 133−9.
30   *ibid.*, p. 191.
31   *Experience and Nature, op. cit.*, p. 4; *Quest for Certainty, op. cit.*, p. 310.
32   See discussion, Chapter 4, under the heading, *Ideas and Thinking*, pp. 68 ff.
33   *Experience and Nature, op. cit.*, p. 4; *Quest for Certainty, op. cit.*, pp. 310−11.
34   *Quest for Certainty, op. cit.*, p. 191.
35   *ibid.*
36   *ibid.*
37   *Experience and Nature, op. cit.*, p. 125.
38   *Quest for Certainty, op. cit.*, p. 83.
39   *Experience and Nature*, p. xii; *Quest for Certainty*, p. 102, 125, 128.
40   *Experience and Nature*, p. xii; *Quest for Certainty*, pp. 102−3.
41   *Quest for Certainty*, pp. 248, 104; *Reconstruction in Philosophy*, pp. 61−4.
42   *Quest for Certainty*, pp. 83, 103.
43   *ibid.*, p. 126.
44   *ibid.*, p. 206.
45   *Experience and Nature, op. cit.*, p. 266.
46   See discussion above, p. 84.
47   *Quest for Certainty, op. cit.*, pp. 87, 90, 94, 104, 134.
48   *ibid.*, p. 92.
49   *ibid.*, pp. 134−6.
50   *ibid.*, pp. 136, 157, 159−60.
51   *ibid.*, p. 163.
52   *Experience and Nature*, p. 4a.
53   *op. cit.*, pp. 109−10.
54   *ibid.*, p. 140.
55   See above, re discussion of man's quest for certainty, desire to control and manipulate nature, role of inquiry − Chapters 2 and 4. Also *Experience & Nature, op. cit.*, p. 7 and *Quest for Certainty, op. cit.*, pp. 100, 104, 131.
56   *Experience and Nature, op. cit.*, pp. 136, 140, 145 ff, 151.
57   *Quest for Certainty, op. cit.*, pp. 131−3, 128.
58   Hence the importance of mathematics. See *Quest for Certainty*, p. 158. See also discussion of *relations*, above pp. 99 ff.
59   See *Quest for Certainty*, pp. 136, 146, 241.
60   e.g. see *Experience and Nature*, pp. 139−42, 144, 149, and *Quest for Certainty*, pp. 106, 129−31.
61   In the pragmatic sense. See above, Chapter 2.
62   *Experience and Nature, op. cit.*, p. 144.
63   *ibid.*, p. 148.
64   *Quest for Certainty, op. cit.*, p. 178. Also see earlier comments re *Dewey and Reality*, (pp. 78−81), and discussion below, p. 105.
65   *Quest for Certainty, op. cit.*, p. 267.
66   *ibid.*, pp. 178−80.
67   *ibid.*, p. 128.
68   *ibid.*, p. 241.

69   *ibid.*, p. 197.
70   *ibid.*, pp. 106, 130, 134, 191, 239.
71   *ibid.*, p. 131.
72   *ibid.*, pp. 128, 104–5.
73   *ibid.*, pp. 104–5.
74   *op. cit.*, pp. 35–45.
75   *ibid.*, p. 42.
76   pp. 86–7.
77   *Quest for Certainty, op. cit.*, pp. 246–50.
78   *ibid.*, pp. 248–9.
79   *ibid.*, p. 248.
80   *ibid.*, pp. 237–41, esp. pp. 240–1.
81   *ibid.*, p. 237.
82   *ibid.*, p. 238.
83   *ibid.*
84   *ibid.*, p. 239.
85   *ibid.*
86   *Experience and Nature, op. cit.*, p. 156.
87   See above, Chapters 2 and 4. Also, *Quest for Certainty, op. cit.*, Chs. 1 and 2.
88   pp. 79–80, 101–2.
89   For example, see his argument in *Quest for Certainty, op. cit.*, pp. 128–9.
90   *Experience and Nature, op. cit.*, pp. 142–6.
91   Dewey illustrated the intimate connection he perceived between knowledge in general and science as the paradigm form of knowledge, by speaking here as though objects of knowledge and objects of science were one and the same thing – which for him they were.
92   Dewey defined a 'tool' as a thing used as a means to produce consequences. *Experience and Nature, op. cit.*, p. 185.
93   *Experience and Nature, op. cit.*, p. 428.
94   *Quest for Certainty, op. cit.*, pp. 24, 36–7, 79, 86, 88, 103–5.
95   *ibid.*, p. 37.
96   e.g. in astronomy one would find it difficult to introduce changes in the behaviour of remote heavenly bodies.
97   *Quest for Certainty, op. cit.*, p. 84.
98   *Experience and Nature, op. cit.*, p. 2a.
99   *ibid.*, p. 133.
100 *Quest for Certainty, op. cit.*, pp. 86, 289.
101 See above, re discussion of inquiry and role played by ideas in inquiry, pp. 68 ff.
102 *Quest for Certainty, op. cit.*, pp. 86–7.
103 e.g. apparatus and instruments to be minutely described, results to be given in full detail, the method of reasoning to be explained, etc. See *Experience and Nature, op. cit.*, p. 36.
104 *ibid.*, p. 30.
105 *ibid.*, pp. 30–1. c/f Campbell's notion of 'truth' and Braithwaite's defence of Peirce – see Chapter 2 above.
106 *Quest for Certainty, op. cit.*, p. 190.
107 See above, Chapter 2, discussion of the instrumentalist notion of 'truth'.

See also *Experience and Nature, op. cit.*, p. 31.

108 *Quest for Certainty, op. cit.*, pp. 190−1. c/f the views of Bernard − see Chapter 3 above.

109 Especially pp. 68 ff.

110 *Quest for Certainty, op. cit.*, pp. 190−1.

111 Dewey's dislike of the traditional philosophical appeal to a form of antecedent Being to explain the workings of nature has been discussed throughout the book.

112 *Quest for Certainty, op. cit.*, pp. 138, 288. This, of course, is a debatable matter, particularly concerning the generation of ideas.

113 *Experience and Nature, op. cit.*, p. 4a. Newton's problem of 'transduction', discussed above, Chapter 4 and in McGuire, *op. cit.*

114 *Experience and Nature, op. cit.*, p. 4a.

115 *Quest for Certainty, op. cit.*, pp. 96−7.

116 *ibid.*, p. 97.

117 or the *intrinsic* tendencies of nature's own operations.

118 *ibid.*, pp. 97−103.

119 *Experience and Nature, op. cit.*, p. 128.

120 *Quest for Certainty, op. cit.*, p. 100.

121 *ibid.*

122 *ibid.*, pp. 99−100.

123 See above, Chapter 4, pp. 67 ff. And scientific knowing becomes the paradigm form of knowing.

124 *Quest for Certainty, op. cit.*, pp. 36−7, 99, 103, 123, 137, 179, 261; *Experience & Nature, op. cit.*, pp. 25, 29. c/f views of Bernard, Chapter 3.

125 Mentioned above, Chapter 4.

126 *Quest for Certainty, op. cit.*, pp. 174.

127 *ibid.*, pp. 123, 103, 137.

128 See above, discussion of the nature of inquiry, Chapters 2 and 4.

129 *Quest for Certainty, op. cit.*, pp. 104, 90, 137, 194. See also discussion above on 'reality' pp. 79, 99−100, 103 ff.

130 *Quest for Certainty, op. cit.*, pp. 123, 178.

131 Dewey's definition of 'real'. See above, pp. 79−80, 100, 103 ff.

132 *Quest for Certainty, op. cit.*, pp. 83, 104−6, 123−5, 131−2.

133 *ibid.*, pp. 173−5; *Experience and Nature, op. cit.*, pp. 4, 155.

134 *Experience and Nature, op. cit.*, p. 381; Dewey's views on logic were discussed above, Chapters 2 and 4.

135 *Quest for Certainty, op. cit.*, p. 174.

136 *Experience and Nature, op. cit.*, p. 7.

137 *Quest for Certainty, op. cit.*, p. 175. See also discussion above on 'truth' and the 'process of inquiry', Chapters 2 and 4.

138 i.e. the doubtful situation leads to a definition of the problem which generates hypotheses which are then tested by experiment and eventually lead to the solution of the problem and a settled situation.

139 However, he did have considerable training in psychology, and also postgraduate training in theoretical physiology.

140 Ostwald, *op. cit.*, p. 43.

141 Dewey, *Experience and Nature, op. cit.*, pp. 128−32.

142   Dewey, *Quest for Certainty, op. cit.*, p. 96.
143   *Quest for Certainty, op. cit.*, pp. 115–20 (esp. pp. 118–19), 142–5.
144   See discussion in Kuhn, T. *The Copernican Revolution*, Vintage Books, 1959, pp. 256–60.
145   *Quest for Certainty, op. cit.*, p. 145.
146   *ibid.*, pp. 202–3. See also discussion of this point in Chapter 2.
147   i.e. since the writings of Mach in the mid-nineteenth century. See above, Chapter 3.
148   *Quest for Certainty, op. cit.*, p. 206.
149   *ibid.*, p. 207.
150   *ibid.*, pp. 211, 277.
151   *ibid.*, p. 248.
152   *Experience and Nature, op. cit.*, p. 148.
153   *ibid.*, pp. 129, 136; *Quest for Certainty, op. cit.*, pp. 135–9.
154   Dewey, *Quest for Certainty, op. cit.*, p. 165.
155   Ostwald, *op. cit.*
156   Campbell, *op. cit.*
157   Sullivan, J. *The Limitations of Science*, Mentor, 1968 (first published 1933).
158   Bridgman, P. *The Logic of Modern Physics*, Macmillan, N.Y., 1960.
159   Reichenbach, *op. cit.*
160   Nagel, *op. cit.*
161   Frank, P. (ed) *Validation of Scientific Theories*, Collier Books, N.Y., 1961, Introduction and pp. 13–26.
162   e.g. quantum mechanics and the computer technique known as total systems analysis. See also the article by White, P. on the role of computers in modern technology in the *National Geographic Magazine*, November, 1970, and the ideas put forward by the sociologist, Moore, W. of which the quotation cited at the beginning of this chapter is a typical example. The essay by Schwab cited in footnote 163 offers further support for this point of view.
163   See Schwab, J. 'The Structure of Disciplines: Meanings and Significances' in Ford and Pugno, *op. cit.*, pp. 6–30.
164   Dewey, *How We Think, op. cit.*, p. v. – a book written for teachers in 1910 and revised in 1933. Dewey held this belief throughout his career. For example, he put forward a similar point of view in 1938. See 'Relation of Science and Philosophy as a basis of Education' in *Problems of Men, op. cit.*, part 2, section 3.

Bibliography

AGRICOLA *De Re Metallica*, trans. Hoover, C & L. Dover, New York, 1950.

AIKEN, H. (ed) *The Age of Ideology*, Mentor, New American Library, New York, 1961.

ALLEN, F. et. al. *Technology and Social Change*, Appleton-Century-Crofts, New York, 1957.

AYER, A. *Language, Truth and Logic*, Victor Gollancz, London, 1967. *The Origins of Pragmatism*, Macmillan, London, 1968.

BACON, F. *Cogitata et Visa* (Thoughts and Conclusions) Original in Spedding, J. et. al. *Works of Francis Bacon*, Vol. III, English Translation in Farrington, B. *The Philosophy of Francis Bacon: Novum Organum*, Bobbs-Merrill, Indianapolis, 1960.

BAKER, A. *Modern Physics and Antiphysics*, Addison-Wesley, London, 1970.

BAYLES, M. (ed) *Contemporary Utilitarianism*, Anchor Books, New York, 1968.

BENJAMIN, A. *Operationism*, Charles C. Thomas, Springfield, Illinois, U.S.A. or Blackwell, Oxford, 1955.

BERNARD, C. *An Introduction to the Study of Experimental Medicine*, Collier Books, New York, 1961.

BERNSTEIN, D. (ed) *On Experience, Nature and Freedom*, Bobbs-Merrill, Indianapolis, 1967.

BLAKE, R. et. al. *Theories of Scientific Method*, University of Washington Press, Seattle, 1966.

BOLTZMANN, L. *Lectures on Gas Theory*, trans. Bush, S., Uni. of California Press, Berkeley, 1964. *Populare Schriften*, Johann Barth, Leipzig, 1905.

BOUTROUX, E. *Natural Law in Science and Philosophy*, trans. Rothwell, F. David Nutt, London, 1914. French edition: *Bibliothèque D'Histoire de La Philosophie de L'Idée de Loi Naturelle dans La Science et La Philosophie Contemporaines*, Librairie Philosophique, J. Vrin, Paris, 1950.

BRAITHWAITE, R. *Scientific Explanation*, Harper Torch Books, New York, 1960.

BRIDGMAN, P. *The Logic of Modern Physics*, Macmillan, New York, 1960.

BRODY, B. (ed) *Readings in the Philosophy of Science*, Prentice Hall, Englewood Cliffs, New Jersey, 1970.

BRONOWSKI, J. *The Common Sense of Science*, Heinemann, London, 1960.

BURNET, J. *Early Greek Philosophy*, Adam and Charles Black, London, 1958.
Greek Philosophy, Macmillan, London, 1960.

CAMPBELL, N. *Foundations of Science*, Dover, New York, 1957.
COHEN, M. *Reason and Nature*, Free Press, Collier – Macmillan, London, 2nd ed. 1964.
Studies in Philosophy and Science, Holt, New York, 1949.
COHEN, M AND DRABKIN, I. *A Source Book in Greek Science*, Harvard Uni. Press, Cambridge, Mass., 1966.
CONANT, J. *Science and Common Sense*, Yale Uni. Press, New Haven, Conn. 1961.
COPLESTON, F. *A History of Philosophy*, Bellarmine Series XIX, Burns and Oates Ltd., London, 1966.

DANTO, A AND MORGENBESSER, S. *Philosophy of Science*, Meridian Books, New American Library, New York, 1960.
DARWIN, C. *On the Origin of the Species by Means of Natural Selection*, Mentor Books, New American Library, New York, 1964.
DEWEY, J. *Democracy and Education*, Macmillan, New York, 1967.
Essays in Experimental Logic, Dover, New York.
Experience & Education, Collier Books, New York, 1963.
Experience & Nature, 2nd ed. Dover, New York, 1958.
How We Think, D. C. Heath & Co., Boston, Mass., 1933.
Influence of Darwin on Philosophy & Other Essays, Indiana Uni. Press. Bloomington, Ind. 1965.
Logic: The Theory of Inquiry, Henry Holt & Co. New York, 1955.
Problems of Men, Philosophy Lib., New York, 1946.
The Quest for Certainty, Capricorn Books, G. P. Putnam's Sons, New York, 1960.
Reconstruction in Philosophy, Beacon Press, Boston, Mass., 1968.
DEWEY J AND BENTLEY, A. *Knowing and the Known*, Beacon Press, Boston, Mass., 1949.
DIJKSTERHUIS, E. *The Mechanisation of the World Picture*, O.U.P. London, 1960.
DUHEM, P. *The Aim and Structure of Physical Theory*, trans. Wiener, P., Princeton Uni. Press, N. J., 1954.
DURRANT, W. *The Story of Philosophy*, Washington Square, Pocket Books, New York, 1961.

FARRINGTON, B. *Greek Science*, Pelican, 1944.
The Philosophy of Francis Bacon, Liverpool Uni. Press. 1964.

FEIGL, H AND MAXWELL, G. (ed) *Minnesota Studies in the Philosophy of Science III* (Explanation, Space and Time), Uni. of Minnesota Press, Minneapolis, 1962.

FORD, G AND PUGNO, L. *The Structure of Knowledge and the Curriculum*, Rand McNally, Chicago, 1965.

FRANK, P. (ed) *The Validation of Scientific Theories*, Collier Books, Macmillan, New York, 1961.

GALLIE, W. *Peirce & Pragmatism*, Harmondsworth, 1952.
Philosophy & the Historical Understanding, Schocken Books, New York, 1964.

GLOVER, T. *The Ancient World*, Pelican, London, 1944.

GOMPERZ, T. *Greek Thinkers*, John Murray, London, 1949.

GUTHRIE, W. *History of Greek Philosophy*, C.U.P., 1969.

HARRÉ, R. (ed) *The Sciences, Their Origins & Methods*, Blackie, Glasgow, 1967.
Scientific Thought (1900–1960), O.U.P., 1969.

HARRÉ, R. *Matter and Method*, Macmillan, London, 1964.
The Philosophies of Science, O.U.P., 1972.
Principles of Scientific Thinking, O.U.P., 1970.

HARTSHORNE, C and WEISS, P. (ed) *Collected Papers of Charles Sanders Peirce*, Harvard Uni. Press, Cambridge, Mass., 1960.

HARVEY, W. *The Circulation of the Blood & Other Writings*, Dent. London, 1952.

HELMHOLTZ, H. *Popular Science Lectures*, trans. Atkinson, E., Dover, New York, 1962.

HERTZ, H. *Principles of Mechanics*, Trans. Jones, D & Walley, J., Dover, New York, 1956.

HIPPOCRATES *Writings*, trans. Jones, W., Loeb Classical Library, Vol. 128–131, Harvard Uni. Press, Cambridge, Mass. 1957.

HOOKE, S. (ed) *John Dewey – Philosopher of Science & Freedom*, Dial Press, New York, 1950.

JAMES, W. *Talks to Teachers*, Longmans, Green & Co., London, 1908.

KNOCKELMANS, J. (ed) *Philosophy of Science*, Free Press, New York, 1968.

KONVITZ, M. and KENNEDY, G. *The American Pragmatists*, Meridian Books, New American Library, New York, 1967.

KUHN, T. *The Copernican Revolution*, Vintage Books, Random House, New York, 1959.

LEWIS, J. *History of Philosophy*, Eng. Uni. Press Ltd, London, 1962.

LOVEJOY, A. *The Great Chain of Being*, Harper Torch Books, Harper &

Row, New York, 1965.
The Thirteen Pragmatisms & Other Essays, Johns Hopkins Uni Press, Baltimore, Maryland, 1963.

MCGUIRE, F. 'Atoms and the "Analogy of Nature" ' in *Studies in the History & Philosophy of Science*, Vol. I, No. 1, May 1970. Macmillan (Journals) London, 1970.

MACINTYRE, A. *A Short History of Ethics*, Routledge and Kegan Paul, London, 1968.

MCKEON, R. *The Basic Works of Aristotle*, Random House, New York, 1941.

MCLAUGHLIN, R. *Theoretical Entities & Philosophical Dualisms*, Ph.D. Thesis, Indiana Uni., 1958.

MADDEN, E. (ed) *The Philosophical Writings of Chauncey Wright*, Liberal Arts Press, Bobbs-Merrill, Indianapolis, 1958.

MAXWELL, G. 'Ontological Status of Theoretical Entities' in Feigl, H. & Maxwell, G. (ed) *Minnesota Studies in the Philosophy of Science III*.

MESTHENE, E. *Technological Change*, Mentor, New American Library, New York, 1970.

MEYERSON, E. *Identity & Reality*, trans. Loewenberg, K. Dover, New York, 1962.

MILL, J. *A System of Logic*, Longmans Green, London, 1884.

MOORE, E. C. *American Pragmatism*, Columbia Uni. Press, New York, 1966.

MOORE, G. *Philosophical Studies*, Routledge & Kegan Paul, London, 1922.

MOORE, W. *Social Change*, Prentice Hall, Englewood Cliffs, N.J., 1969.

MORAVCSIK, J. (ed) *Aristotle*, Macmillan, London, 1968.

NAGEL, E. *The Structure of Science*, Routledge & Kegan Paul, London, 1961.

NAGEL, E. et. al. (ed) *Logic, Methodology, and Philosophy of Science*, Stanford Uni. Press, California, 1962.

NOSSAL, G. 'Medical Research & the Future of Man' in *University of Melbourne Gazette*, May, 1970.

O'CONNOR, D. (ed) *A Critical History of Western Philosophy*, Free Press of Glencoe, New York, 1965.

OSTWALD, W. *Natural Philosophy*, trans. Seltzer, T. Williams and Norgate, London, 1911.

PASSMORE, J. *A Hundred Years of Philosophy*, Penguin, Harmondsworth, 1968.

PEARSON, K. *The Grammar of Science*, Dent, London, 1911.

PEIRCE, C. S. *Collected Papers*, see Hartshorne, C. *Essay in the Philosophy of*

Science (Tomas, V. ed) Bobbs-Merrill, Indianapolis, 1957.

PHILLIPS, D.C. 'The Idea of Evolution in Educational Thought' in French, E. (ed) *Melbourne Studies in Education, 1966*, M.U.P.
'John Dewey and the Organismic Archetype' in Selleck, R. (ed) *Melbourne Studies in Education, 1971*, M.U.P.
Organicism and its Influence on the Philosophical and Educational Writings of John Dewey, Ph.D. Thesis, Melbourne University, 1968.

PLATO *Timaeus*, trans. Cornford, F. & published under the title, *Plato's Cosmology*, Routledge and Kegan Paul, London, 1966.

POINCARÉ, H. *Science and Method*, trans. Maitland, F., Dover, New York, 1959.
The Value of Science, trans. Halsted, B., Dover, New York, 1958.

POPPER, K. *Conjectures & Refutations*, Routledge & Kegan Paul, London, 1969.
The Logic of Scientific Discovery, Hutchinson, London, 1959.

RATNER, J. (ed) *Intelligence in the Modern World*, Random House, New York, 1939.

REICHENBACH, H. *The Rise of Scientific Philosophy*, Uni. of California Press, Berkeley, 1968.

RUSSELL, B. *History of Western Philosophy*, Allen & Unwin, London, 1961.
Our Knowledge of the External World, Allen & Unwin, London, 1929.

SCHILPP, P. A. (ed) *The Philosophy of John Dewey*, Library of Living Philosophers, Tudor Publishing Co., New York, 1951, 2nd Edition.

SCHNEIDER, H. *A History of American Philosophy*, New York, 1946.

SELLARS, W. 'Language of Theories' in Feigl, H & Maxwell, G. *Current Issues in the Philosophy of Science*, Holt, Rinehart and Winston, New York, 1961.
'Scientific Realism or Irenic Instrumentalism' in Cohen, R. & Wartofsky, M. (eds) *Boston Studies in Philosophy of Science*, Vol. II, Humanities Press, New York, 1965.

SMART, J. *Between Science & Philosophy*, Random House, New York, 1968.
Philosophy & Scientific Realism, Routledge and Kegan Paul, London, 1963.

SOPHOCLES *Antigone*, in *The Theban Plays*, Penguin, Harmondsworth, 1964.

SPEDDING, J. et al. *The Works of Francis Bacon*, various Publishers London, 1857.

STALLO, J. *Concepts and Theories of Modern Physics* (Bridgman, P. ed), Harvard Uni. Press, Cambridge, Mass., 1960.

STRAWSON, P. *Introduction to Logical Theory*, Methuen & Co., London, 1960.

SULLIVAN, J. *The Limitations of Science*, Mentor, New American Library, New York, 1968.

THAYER, H. *The Logic of Pragmatism*, Humanities Press, New York, 1952. *Meaning and Action*, Bobbs-Merrill, Indianapolis, 1968.
TOULMIN, S. *The Philosophy of Science*, Hutchinson, London, 1953. *The Uses of Argument*, Cambridge Uni. Press. London, 1958.

VAIHINGER, H. *The Philosophy of 'As If'* trans. Ogden, G., International Library of Psychology, Philosophy, Scientific Method, London, 1924.
VESALIUS, A. *On the Human Brain*, trans. Singer, C., O.U.P., 1952.

WARNOCK, G. *Contemporary Moral Philosophy*, Macmillan, London, 1967.
WHITE, M. *The Age of Analysis*, Mentor Books, New American Library, New York, 1960.
WHITE, P. T. 'Behold the Computer Revolution', *National Geographic Magazine*, Vol. 138, No. 5, Nov., 1970, Nat. Geog. Soc., Washington, D.C.
WIENER, P. *Evolution & The Founders of Pragmatism*, Torch Books, Harper & Row, New York, 1965.
WITTGENSTEIN, L. *The Blue and the Brown Books*, Blackwell, Oxford, 1969, 2nd edition.

ZIMAN, J. *Public Knowledge*, Cambridge University Press, London, 1968.

Index